The Elderly Traveler's Guide to Advanced Study

Thomas Brahana

Bilbo Books Publishing
www.BilboBooks.com

ISBN- 978-1-7326180-8-4
ISBN- 1-7326180-9-7

Printed in the United States of America

Dedication

This book is dedicated to the concept of

Growing Old Together,

and to my wife Mary Ann,

without whom I could not have

studied this concept.

TABLE OF CONTENTS

Introduction

This book had its origins in two letters I wrote to my father from Yugoslavia in 1972. My youngest daughter, Joan, called them my "Epic Letters."

We traveled regularly over the years, but I did not write the minutiae of traveling again until 1978 when I composed a letter to my daughter Elizabeth, which I never mailed, but has been saved in my study.

I continued composing unsent "Epic Letters" to my children: to Joan in 1988, to Patrick in 1989, to Danny in 1990. At this time, having run out of children, I began to refer to my "letters" as journals, which are just letters to my future self.

The writing style evolved over time. My wife, Mary Ann, and I found ourselves referring to the journals to recall details blissfully erased by time. There are now some two dozen of them.

On reading an advertisement of the publishers, Bilbo Books, in a Town & Gown playbill, I conceived the idea of this book.

The material as written, while understandable to the addressees, needs explanation to make it sensible to a wider audience. This has been added.

The book needed a theme. Two suggested themselves. First, our trips had some aspects of the standard old American notion of the Grand Tour, spread over decades in our retirement years. The second theme was the comparison of cultures, mine the culture of Athens, Georgia, and what I brought to it — the others, cultures of the countries visited, as transmitted by the things seen and the people encountered, is recorded in the journals, and now this book.

The culture of a society is strongly time-dependent. It can change radically overnight, on the eruption of war, for example, or political or economic changes. This is sometimes mentioned in the journals that have been included here, written between 1988 and 1997.

I remember the Reagan and Clinton years as having been relatively tranquil and prosperous. The tourism industry flourished abroad.

As a traveler, I am always a mathematician. It's my profession, and has informed my observations in the book, as well as everything else. I've decided not to use as many acronyms as most mathematicians would. We love acronyms. That being said, there are two which I can't not include: CCM and LLLP.

The CCM is my code for Card-Carrying Mathematician. There's no actual card, and yet my being a CCM informs my worldview. LLLP is the Life-Long Learning Process.

One description of mathematics is that it is a language whose purpose is the expression of certainty. This language is independent of the languages one uses in spoken communication: English, French, Russian, Chinese, etc. Thus, the mathematical sentence, "3X=6" means exactly the same thing in each of them. A mathematician at Time T should be sufficiently fluent in this language to express himself clearly about the evolved mathematics that exists at Time T. So, a mathematician uses sentences from Mathematical Language to analyze situations in real life, to the extent that he is able.

In envisioning the procedure for getting my book done, I am called to the procedure of Mark Twain in writing his autobiography. Towards the end of that monumental epic he used the method of writing the thoughts that sprung into his mind when he encountered current sources (newspaper articles, conversations,...), which set off a train of thought. My variation is writing down the thoughts I have in reading the journals themselves (as they are letters to my future self), written while traveling abroad.

It is wrong to compare myself to Mark Twain. But it is also wrong not to admit that I have learned from a great teacher, like Mister Twain, in my own personal LLLP.

Among other things, Twain interpreted the Civil War for the American people in his work – *Huckleberry Finn*, etc. There is a very lovely passage in his autobiography, describing a letter from a Virginian, the effect that his *Innocents Abroad* had on certain Civil War survivors who were trying to cope with abandoning the conviction that God had been on their side.

If one lives to be elderly, and one attempts to tell the story of his life, one often assembles a scrapbook of memories of events (which may or may not have happened). An important part of my Life-Long Learning Process is to read great autobiographies. Mark Twain's, Jane Fonda's *Prime Time*, selected W. B. Yeats poems, various autobiographies, histories and the sequence of Picasso's paintings are some such examples which have affected me personally.

That a person's life has definitive stages was recognized three thousand years ago in the Riddle of the Sphinx. That one's Life-Long Learning Process has stages is well-accepted by those who think about this subject. One of these stages is centered on the time of retirement. At that time, one's attention is freed from concentrating on the mundane, day-to-day details of supporting oneself and one's family. This freedom allows for the concentration on aspects of the LLLP that have previously been left unexplored, such as the foreign travel for education and entertainment which I used as the basis for this book.

The essence of your identity is what makes you "You." Your youness is something only you have. Yes, that sounds wildly simplistic, but it's also undeniably true. In order to live to be elderly, and thus to be able to experience elderly travel, the key is to have a well-nourished "Feel Good." When you lose your "Feel Good," you are not long for this world.

As a mathematician (CCM), the story I would like to tell begins like this:

Invoking Axiom 2 (cogito, ergo sum), leads to the existence of the LLLP on the part of an individual. The LLLP of that individual has certain stages, which can be described and delineated. The one telling this story, in this case a CCM in the final stage of his life, had landed at certain conclusions about the world, due to the variables of his personal LLLP. The particular CCM is the constant in the grand equation of life and the places he visits contain many different variables.

The journals (letters I wrote to my future self) are too bulky to be fully contained in this book. I have cut a lot, always searching for the essentials with which to create a narrative story. I said I wouldn't use any more acronyms, but as a CCM, I have to include NQs (Natural Questions). NQs came up all the time in my travels. The rule which governed my inclusion of certain information has come from my asking myself whether specific observations provide adequate answers to the NQs I had when traveling, including heavy doses of genealogy. Others came from NQs I had asked myself for years, but which have become clearer with the benefit of earned hindsight.

Finally, in conclusion, I reach the fact that I am content with the approach of a CCM.

On Genealogy

"OHHH, *THAT'S* WHY I'M LIKE THAT." This is one of my biggest revelations from a lifetime of genealogical research. I set out to discover who my ancestors were, and, in the process, I figured out quite a bit about myself.

Perhaps the biggest step occurred when I was reading my mother's old poems and discovered there was a great deal in my outlook on life that I thought I had inherited from my father, but had, in fact, inherited from my mother.

It wasn't until, when in Canada I discovered that my mother had been the captian of her basketball team, that I connected the dots on a small family mystery. My mother was a calm, very together woman, but she always got very excited when we'd listen to a basketball game on the radio. I hadn't understood it as a child, but upon discovering her past, it made sense.

That is why everyone should take the time to explore genealogy.

A man's life has stages, a fact recognized for several centuries, as indicated by The Riddle of the Sphinx. (Riddle: What has four legs in the morning, two at noon, and three at twilight? Answer: Man. Man, who crawls as a child, walks as an adult, and uses a cane in old age.)

Equally, an individual's LLLP has stages, and in the stage of retirement one becomes more interested in genealogy, the stories of those who contributed to one's gene pool.

There is a divide in this study. The methods and information obtained about those we have actually known, and those we have not, are different.

That's my story.

The Lure of Mathematics

A four dimensional space
In a nine dimensional space
Has points and lines and surfaces
That maybe compared to a similar base.

If you draw a circle
Around a bug or a worm
He must cross that circle to be free
But a bird can use another dimension
And fly away, you see.

Everyone knows a three dimensional space.
A rat in a cage has a snap
If you give him a fourth kind of space
He can get out of his trap.

Why would a person spend a life
Washing dishes, cleaning rooms, serving meals,
When Theory of Groups stretches the mind
And its secret reveals.

YUGOSLAVIA & ITALY

Yugoslavia was created following World War I by representatives of the victors, who used economic considerations to firm a country of size large enough to survive alongside Austria, Hungary, Greece, Italy, etc. History was ignored. World War II created the tensions which eventually led to the dissolution into more or less tribal lines.

#1—April 9, 1972

Letter home from Yugoslavia to his father (which, along with advice from Jane Fonda about good habits to get into when aging, he credits as his impetus for the beginning of his journaling journey)

Dear Dad,

It is a dampish Sunday morning in Zagreb, and I came down to my office to write you about our Italian trip. Before I write you the details, let me say that I cannot imagine anything more beautiful. Before we went, I hadn't thought much about the fact that Florence is where Mother was when she died, but when the thought occurred to me from time to time I didn't push it away. That was part of the trip, mixed in with lots of other things which I will now try to write about.

Zagreb, Croatia

Early Monday morning we got up and ate breakfast and hopped in the Fiat. By now we know some of the simple things, so in no time we were barreling on down the road to Ljubljana – a little apprehensive – it isn't possible to make reservations in Italy from here – but it was a nice day, and things are beginning to green up.

We had decided to skip the Trieste border crossing, which is very busy and commercial, and go over the mountains to Nova Gorica. It was the better choice, because even though the road is narrower and has more twists, there was relatively little traffic and no trucks at all. We went through half a dozen little Alpine villages, pleasant places, half Yugoslavian, half Austrian. There were a very few snow patches, lots of little yellow and white flowers, green meadows, pines and hardwoods. After a while we had a real climb over the ridge that extends along the Adriatic, and we could see the valley, and Nova Gorica laid out below. Gorizia has an old castle which we could see from up there.

We slithered on down the side of the hill, crossed the border in less than a minute, saw a nice green Autostrada sign, and drove on past the Exchange, forgetting that I barely had enough Lira for the toll on the Autostrada.

It wasn't noon yet.

A couple of years ago we read an article about Aquileia, which was a very important Roman town at the top of the Adriatic, where they found some really great early Christian mosaics under the floor of the church. So we drove on down to see if we could find it. Instead of turning right on the Autostrada toward Venice, we went straight about 5 miles to the shore. Pretty soon we could see what was obviously the church, so we drove through some narrow streets, and came to the church, with its square. There were some people there, 20 cars, a bus or two. It was a holiday, the day after Easter, there were bunches of nice young Italian youngsters there on excursion. The sun was bright and Mediterranean. Our mob was hungry, but we spent about half an hour looking at those mosaics. There wasn't a picnic table in sight. As we drove out of Aquileia we saw some very inviting Roman ruins, but I was still a little reluctant to lay out lunch without knowing the ground rules. So in 20 minutes or so we pulled off the Autostrada into a service area, and had our ham and Easter Eggs and bread and cheese and Dvojni-C and Coke off the hood of the car, under the picture of an attractive red-headed girl holding the nozzle of the gasoline pump. It was really kind of nice – their service areas are still pretty clean, lots of grass and new trees.

On to Venice.

We drove on the causeway and got to the parking area. What a mob! Italians like to go to Venice the day after Easter. All of those stands that say Hotel Reservations had lines with people waving their arms. There was a line a block long waiting to go in the parking garage, and I toured the lot and there wasn't a space anywhere. Panic. So I got in the line for the parking and after a while we got a slot way in the top. We left the children, went down to the booth in the Garage that said Hotel Reservations and said we wanted a reservation. The guy said, "What Hotel?" and Mary Ann fished around in her purse and found the name of a place that one of her buddies had given her, and said Hotel Flora. The guy dialed the phone, handed it to her. Horns tooting, cars gunning by, people all over. But we got a room, expensive, "We'll hold it for an hour."

So we took off back upstairs, got our suitcases, couldn't get the elevator, finally got down and located the vaporetta. No Lira at all now. A holiday. We couldn't buy tickets for the boat. So Mary Ann and I started out. We asked the girl in the Hertz and she threw up her hands. I went in the parking garage and asked a guy who wasn't doing anything where and he said here, and I exchanged $10. Back to the vaporetta. What a mob! But we pushed in with our suitcases and our children, and the belief that our stop was 12.

We'd lost our sunshine, but it was still pretty nice. By this time we began to worry, "Did the hotel really mean an hour?" But we chugged along, squeezing under a bridge or two, and piled off with the mob at St. Mark's. And I didn't know whether I could afford to have the luggage carried. After some indecision the guy said it would cost 1000 Lira, and I said okay. It was a bargain, because he knew where the hotel was and I didn't.

Off we went down the street, over some bridges, down a shop-lined street to an alley with a little sign that said Hotel Flora. We went back in, and it was clear that it was a good place. There was a little garden. Our room was beautiful – perhaps the nicest I have ever slept in. A dozen big pieces of inlaid furniture – some fabric wall covering – fine prints and pictures – the lot. Across the garden was the house in which Giuseppe Verdi composed the opera "Othello."

We rested a little. I was really a little distracted. But after 10 minutes off to St. Mark's. It was only two blocks away – only one bridge to cross. The square was jammed with Italians. Only a few Americans, Germans, English and French. Thousands of just ordinary Italians: soldiers, sailors, families, young people, courting people, old people, all talking and eating and enjoying themselves. Twenty thousand people.

St. Mark's Cathedral, Venice

Saint Mark's is very impressive. We walked around inside for a while, and then out in the square again. Then we walked around in the old city, keeping our eyes out for a cheap place to eat. We found one with a fixed price menu that was in our class. Later at 8:00 PM we went back there and it was pretty good – not great. Good pasta, veal cutlets, wine and an orange. For less than $2 apiece.

We walked around after supper for a while – down to the canal, The Bridge of Sighs, but it was beginning to blow a little so we went home to bed.

The next morning we opened the dining room at 7:30. Another fine room. We ate our rolls and drank our coffee and tea and butter – scraped up every crumb and started off for the Gallery of the Academy. By this time we had found a useful guidebook.

When we got there, the Gallery wasn't open, so we kept walking. The Academy Bridge across the Grand Canal gives some very nice views of the houses along the canal. There's a big church every 100 feet in Venice. So we walked for an hour or so, found the second most important church, and got back to the Gallery at 10, opening time.

It is full of the old stuff, the Madonnas, Pietas, etc. We were there until almost noon. It is hard to reconstruct Venice's galleries after Florence. But they are powerful, even so.

Then we went back to our hotel, and planned the rest of the day. The Ducal Palace, and then out of the high rent district. We found a pizza place, had lunch. Mary Ann had compari, which puckered her lips. The pizza was good, and off we went.

The Duke's Palace is very nice. There are tremendous rooms. It is hard for me to imagine their being used functionally. The boys liked the armor. We went across the bridge into the prison. It's pretty awful there. What a contrast! Then out into the sunshine, the square, the trip to the parking building. That was pleasant – we stood on the deck where we could see everything. We unblocked the car, and off we went.

We decided to try Padua…on the basis of, "A gentleman well born in

Basilica di Sant'Antonio da Padova, Padua, Italy

Padua." So we peeled off the Autostrada, etc., again slightly apprehensive. We kept toward the center of the city, and finally saw one that might be our type. The rooms were like an American hotel, newly remodeled, 20th century depressive. But it was what we wanted and 1/2 the price of the night before.

We didn't know it but the two best cathedrals of Padua were less than a block away – and a big park, which the boys needed. So we walked, peeked in one, went in the other, as the dusk came on us. The boys ran around — Chased each other while we sat on a bench. The big cathedral had really been messed up in the war. Just a few walls left. But they had it all back, a huge building really. But they lost all of their frescoes and some important art.

Then we started to look for supper about 7:00. It was a mistake — Too early. Patrick was almost wild. There were plenty of trattoria, they just weren't ready to go. This sort of thing has a way of solving itself with time, and we went into a nice businesslike, non-tourist restaurant where no one spoke English. We had goulash and chicken, beer and strawberries. Very nice.

We walked home, through downtown Padua, past some of the University, and went to bed.

When we woke up in the morning there was a fine misty rain. We had breakfast in The American Bar. No windows. Then I went out down the little street where I parked my car, wondering how much of it would still be there. It was all there, and I started it up and proceeded to get lost. One-way streets and bad angles. Pretty soon I was really lost. But I made a bunch of turns on the basis of heading into the type of neighborhood the hotel was in, and finally came on it from the other side. Fortunately they were advertising a nude movie on the side of the building, so I knew I was home. I'd forgotten the name of the place if I ever knew it. Needless to say I was expected.

Off we went, into the rain. It wasn't a bad ride, occasionally it would give the impression that it was going to clear up. Then black again. When we got into the mountains a downpour.

When we got to Florence it was drizzling. We decided to try the Auto Club for help in getting a room. They weren't any help. They didn't have a map. We tried to call the Bencista, but it was no good because we don't speak any Italian. So we took off towards the center of the city. We drove along the river until we got pushed back in by one-way streets.

Finally we saw a Tourist Agency. Shortly afterwards we saw a parking space. Things were critical, since it was noon, closing time. But a nice boy in the tourist agency took us in hand. He called the Bencista — No luck. We told him about what we could afford, and he got us a place 20% more expensive. I wasn't too happy and said, "Well, book us for one night," so he said he'd get us a less expensive hotel. He did — A 3rd Classer, one block from the Duomo, really an OK place. I had to park my car at the train station, but that didn't really bother me. So we unloaded, and I went and parked.

Then we ate. Sandwiches. The high school hang-out. The Lycee Galileo was across the street.

After lunch we went to the Baptistery and the Cathedral. It was 3:00 and it started to pour. I got soaked, although I had my umbrella. The Cathedral is great. We went to the basement, to see the archeological excavating, mainly because it was out of the rain. Very intellectually stimulating.

Then we went back to the hotel. Our room was large, clean, with a bath. The children didn't have a bath, and were a mess. The street below, Via Martelli, was busy until pretty late.

I decided to go look for a place to eat. I walked and walked. The beautiful warm, wet dusk, churches, hospitals, shops, city buildings, restaurants, bookstores...I found a fine, cheap cafeteria for students. Decided against it. Finally after making a large circle I found a cafeteria in our class not too far. I went and picked up the mob. They were ready to eat, as usual. I had sliced turkey, cold string beans, greens and an orange pop. I talked with an American boy and his wife, who were celebrating his graduation from something. Their baby was cooing nicely in her arms.

Then out for gelato, and home to bed.

The next morning when we woke up the sun was shining. We decided, on the basis of information in the back of our guidebook, to go to the Academy to see David. We got there at 9:00 sharp, after eating a leisurely breakfast (that is, apology for a breakfast), and it wasn't open until 10:00. So off we walked to the Pitti Palace, across the Ponte

Vecchio. I took the boys, Mary Ann and Joan went to the hotel to drop off some purchases (tea, for presents. Communist tea isn't that good.). The boys and I went down to the bridge and across and looked into some shops. We made a bad connection with Joan and Mary Ann.

So then we went through the Palace. It is tremendous. I liked the Queen Elizabeth, Cromwell, the big pictures, everything. There was a mob. School children. Tourists — German, American. Everywhere. The boys were beginning to flag. There was a beautiful table inlayed with different birds. The throne room is impressive, and the big banquet room. The big blue Chinese vases are nice. Brought back by Venetian traders, I guess.

Then we went out to our hotel, and off to a pizza place we had spotted on the other side of the bridge. We got lemonade at 50 cents a glass. One of the 2 or 3 times we got tagged. Then we went to the Uffizi. Seeing those two galleries on the same day was madness. Like getting hit on the head with a 2-by-4. There was a special exhibit of Durer engravings at the beginning. Very fine. I liked the famous paintings in the Uffizi best – the paintings of the man and his wife in the piece of furniture — the Boticellis — "The Adoration of the Magi." Perhaps because I didn't have enough time to make independent selections, and gravitated to those I recognized. After going through 3 or 4 rooms my mind would boggle, and I'd go out on the sun porch to rest my mind. It's no rest — There is as much there — On the ceilings — There is a complete art gallery in a strip around the top of the wall, portraits of Medici's and their buddies — And major statues. The length of it.

We left about 3:30 and staggered back to our hotel. I decided to see how my car was down at the train station. The boys stayed at the hotel and read. Mary Ann went to look at the Medici Tomb. I walked and walked...down to the train station, to the big Fiat place to see about shipping my car home. On the way back I bought some apples and oranges and strawberries to eat in our room. It was nice to wander around in that beautiful town in the late spring afternoon.

When I got back it was almost time to go to supper. Mary Ann had spotted a reasonable-looking fixed price place for 1000 Lira (now about $1.80). So we went there. The food was good – I had Chianti, boiled beef, peas, and bullion. Just as we were finishing a big disturbance broke out at the next table. Probably some boy who didn't have money was trying to leave without paying. It was a family restaurant. Momma came out of the kitchen and almost knocked the boy down. Fortunately we were finished, so we waited a little, paid and left. The disturbance was still in progress.

Palazzo Vecchio, Florence, Italy

So we looked at the Palazzo Vecchio, bought some ice cream, and went home.

The next morning we shaped up at opening time at breakfast. Joan, the boys and I had scheduled the climb of the Campanile Tower. Mary Ann doesn't like stairs. It was a beautifully bright, clear day. I took my maps and located everything. Fiesole was very easy to see. The city is almost gold. The cathedral is ivory. A wonderful sequence of impressions. Everything perfect, from micro to macro to global.

Then we went to see the Academy. This time we got there at 10 AM., and there was a mob. The person in line ahead of me got 63 tickets. Also, probably the person behind me. Tours all over the place. Even so, the gallery can stand it. Even seeing it that way has its charm. I got mad at an ugly American who was flashing away flash bulbs after the guard told him not to, signs on the wall, etc.

Then we went out and had another pizza. Cokes for 20 cents. It was good.

It was still a bright, clear, sunny, warm day. The boys were really filled up with museums. So we decided to walk to the garden across the river up on the hill where you can see the whole city. It was tremendous. We walked from our hotel past the Cathedral, the Palazzo Vecchio, across the Ponte Vecchio, along the river for a couple of bridges, and then up through the garden to the top of the hill. There were lots of things to watch, a man sculling in the river, the dredging (to avoid another flood I suppose), the lilacs and flowers. It was shirt-sleeve weather, and while the season is starting, we had a bench on top to ourselves with the complete view for more than an hour without being in anyone's way. There were always benches empty, and at times there was no one else in the portion of the park where we were. The boys calmed down. Joan was rapturous, and so were her mother and father.

I decided to change some money, and take a few of the tickets off my windshield in the parking lot, so I went first by myself. I decided to check the working hours of a bank I'd seen for the extra 5 Lira/$. It was open from 4-4:45, and I passed it at 3:45 on the way to get my passport at the hotel. Very smooth.

So I got some Lira and off to the train station. The guy at the car knew me by now. He thought it was funny that I paid every day. He had a big handlebar mustache. Back through the city. A quick look in the Baptistery again. The Florentine women are beautiful.

Off to supper. I voted for a fixed-pricer of 1300 Lira, to see if there is a difference. It definitely was better – lasagna with green noodles, veal cutlet, string beans and fruit salad and lemon pop. The lasagna was excellent. It was a small basement, half-filled, 4 tables with Americans and one with Tedeschi.

We walked around in the moonlight until 10, hating to have to go.

We left a call for 6 AM. I got dressed and Patrick and I went for the car. The sun was coming up, but it was not as clear as the day before. Very nice in the cool, faintly-misty morning past the Cathedral. There wasn't much traffic, but the streets weren't empty. My mind was occupied with the problem of driving back to the hotel on the one-way streets. (When the time came there were enough signs, although the route was a pure maze, turn at every corner.) We got to the station, after making my usual detour by a church, St. Margaret's perhaps. The parking lot attendants were all feeding the pigeons on a canvas. They could pick them up while they were feeding them, and toss them in the air. Probably all of this interest has an ulterior motive. So I brought my car back and we slithered over to the hotel. Everyone was more or less waiting. We bought a bag of rolls and oranges and were off by 7, hunting for the Autostrada.

After the usual anxiety we found it, and were purring on down the road, back through the Apennines in a mist but no rain. The plain around Bologna was beautiful, flowers on all of the apples, pears and cherries. Big orchards, espaliered trees, miles of them.

We stopped for a coffee break at 10 o'clock. I don't really like those places but they are practical. I had espresso, which I don't dislike. But I really like the way Yugoslavians fix coffee. They make a sort of paste that varies in density from top to bottom, and it is a great art knowing when to stop. It's also about ½ sugar. No cream or milk. You drink a small cup. It does you a lot of good, in the sense that you don't sit around wondering whether or not you've just had any coffee.

They had a small market – wine, brandy, whiskey, gin, and soda crackers and chocolates — And I saw the biggest bottle of Coke I've ever seen, which I bought. The people there thought it was hilarious.

Then off up the road. We crossed back at Nova Gorica, just as fast, and then proceeded to lose the road. We stopped at a supermarket to buy picnic stuff, relieved to be back where people speak our language (Yugoslavia). Then we stopped for gas and got redirected, in Yugoslavian, and drove for about 15 minutes and stopped for lunch beside the road. There was a nice village on the side of the mountain about a mile away — red tile roofs, tan stucco walls, a few painted in pastels. There were newly-plowed fields and a few flowering trees, and a good view of the ridge we were about to climb.

Then off down the road. It was a wonderfully clear afternoon. When we finally got some height, we could see the Alps in good shape, the first time I've seen them along here. We retraced our steps — Through Ljubljana, along the Sava and Krka, onto the Panonian Plain, and into our stomping ground.

We got home at 5 on Saturday afternoon, in time for Mary Ann to go to our neighborhood store for groceries. It was great.

I didn't really mean to write such a long letter, but I got caught up in it. I am making the boys make a diary. We have enjoyed Elizabeth's so much.

I hope you are OK. I think you are doing fine with the mailing. We need Mary Ann's W-2 form from H & R Block, but don't know whether it has been sent anywhere.

We think about you a lot. You will have to take a long time to read my letter.

All my love,

Tom

YUGOSLAVIA

The dissolution of Yugoslavia was delayed by Tito, who made a sincere effort to unite the tribes, but after his death, it was not long before the country split into the former and modern Croatia, Serbia, Bosnia, Montenegro and Slovenia. My year was at the end of Tito's tenure as dictator.

#2—(another letter home from Yugoslavia, almost a month later)

May 5, 1972

Dear Dad,

WE HAD ANOTHER ELEGANT TRIP OVER THE LAST WEEKEND. Different, but exciting, and fun all of the way. I hope I haven't waited too long to write so that it had faded in my mind, but I doubt it. At any rate, I will try to tell you about it.

Last weekend was the May Day holiday here, and that is one of the biggest holidays in communist countries. We had Saturday-Tuesday off, and had planned a trip to the Adriatic, and had even made some reservations, at a Hotel in Split.

We left very early Saturday morning. It was a good time, since most people from Zagreb were on the road by noon on Friday, and the traffic was not bad. The weather was beautiful, crisp and clear after two weeks of rain and drizzle. We had a bag of things to eat in the car as a breakfast substitute. Oranges, sweetbread, a thermos of coffee. You can't get breakfast anywhere if you want it. So we were off, through Karlovac, a town we are rather familiar with, along the National Park at Plitvice, where the water was high. We didn't stop because we had ambitious plans. There were some cars, but the traffic wasn't too bad. We could see the various waterfalls, and the lakes were bright green and it was frustrating to have to pass them by. There are a lot of hairpin turns through the park, and there was a little snow in the shady places, but the foliage was much thicker than a month ago when we spent the day there. As you leave the park the road follows a stream, clear and fast, full of melted snow. There are a few houses, a mill or two, but the impression is very much that of a park. When I talked to the American Consul at the PTA meeting he said it was the best fishing in all of Europe, in the streams that fed into the lakes. He had been the week before and had caught 12 big trout. You are allowed to keep only 3.

After the park there is a stretch of pretty good road, through some backwoods country. It is pleasant to drive through, and reminds me more of the mountains in Pennsylvania and New York that we saw on our way to Montreal than anything I can think of at the moment.

Joan wasn't with us. She had arranged to visit Anglika in Lika, which is where we were, and so we were on the lookout for the turn we would take to Prozor when we came back. We came onto a very pleasant, wide valley, with a swollen river meandering through it. A tributary of the Lika, and this goes through Prozor. So we knew our future turn off. The road was somewhat like the road to Bakersfield. I wouldn't know the difference, but the comparison exists.

As we drove along we could see the big ridge we had to cross to get to the sea, just as a couple of weeks ago. It was about 10 o'clock, and we worked our way up, a twenty or thirty minute climb, a mile or so between sharp turns, to a five mile straight stretch in the high country. There is another national park, associated with a mountain whose name I can't remember. There is a new tourist hotel, and a ruined village nearby, with a roofless church of grey stone, and some other ruined buildings. There is a small cluster of new houses off to the side, perhaps they work in the hotel or something.

We went through some more sheep grazing land and there were some backpackers, who indicated they would rather ride, and soon we came to the high point, from which you can see the Adriatic. It is spectacular from there — The Island of Pag is down below. It is completely bare. The Italians stripped off all of the trees during World War II. The Adriatic coast really suffered, and has not been repopulated. In order to get something started the communists allow people to build summer houses on the Adriatic, and many of our friends have them.

We stopped for a moment on the top, and the wind was very strong. Twenty or thirty miles an hour. The island is light reddish brown, the sea very blue. You couldn't see the waves from up there, and the coast is grey rock with some green pines and scrub growth.

Then the road drops very rapidly to the sea. Three thousand feet down and two miles horizontal is my guess. When we got down there was a big difference in the temperature. Ten or fifteen degrees.

There is a little town at the bottom, Karlobag. We ate there in the fall. It was bustling today: busses, young people, a recently-smashed car on the dock, ferry boats, and a crowd waiting for one. Everybody had a May Day look, a holiday, the real opening of the summer philosophy.

But we still wanted to get to our luncheon appointment (it turned out to be dinner) in Nin. It was about 60 or 70 miles away, and the road isn't extremely fast.

We drove along the Adriatic. It is a beautiful drive. There are some parts of the road that are full of sharp turns, and considerable ups and downs. But there are really many exciting views, of inlets and villages, towns across the sea on islands. There are always people, walking home from the store, tending sheep, walking along with donkeys. After twenty miles or so the road cuts back in. It is still pretty wild, like the Mid Cape Highway, more or less.

We got to Zadar. Nin is about 10 miles north of Zadar. We had instructions on how to get to Nin, but there aren't any road signs, and in an old town the main road may have an inauspicious beginning. So we managed to get lost, not seriously, and rode along the harbor for an extra mile or two. We had a map, and tried to figure out a way to go cross lots, but this is not a European phenomenon. Finally we found the road, 15 minutes lost, and were riding along, through the tank maneuver area, some cultivated fields, vineyards, a very old small church on a little hill in the middle of a field, until we came through a little town, relatively new, obviously the suburb of Nin.

The Island of Nin, Yugoslavia

Nin is an island, and we went over the bridge. The road goes by the old gate, you have to make a detour 20 feet or so, around the gate. These old gates are more like houses than gates. Our instructions were to drive to the center of town and stop and they would know we were there and come out to see us. We drove to the center of town, 5 or 6 blocks, just past the cathedral, and stopped. We were in front of Zlata's mother's house. Their 5 year old son Dubrovko came out of a courtyard, and soon Ivan was there. He came out from under his car, where he had been repairing his tailpipe. We were a little early.

It was a beautiful warm Mediterranean day. We went through a small passage to the courtyard. Things were in some disorder from the construction. Some stairs were being built. But almost every house in Yugoslavia has some construction in progress. The courtyard is very nice. There are grapes on wires across the top, and they told us that in the summers they were like a roof. The courtyard was, say, 50 feet by 35 feet, filled with plants, an outside staircase, a balcony. Two families live there, Zlata's brother, and her mother and perhaps an aunt. There was formerly a restaurant in one of the big rooms, not now in use. We met Zlata's mother, her brother and sister-in-law, and a slew of children, mostly small. There was a little dismay that dinner wasn't ready, but we really wanted to see the town, and Ivan took us out to show it to us.

About a block away there is a very old church, called Sveta Croce, or whatever. It is the oldest church with a roof in Yugoslavia, from 800. Nin was the capitol of Croatia at the time of King Tomaslav, and he was crowned somewhere in Nin, probably there at that church. They have patched it up some, and it looks pretty good, but it is not in use now. It is not very large, and is built like a cross. There was a wooden barrier on the door, but it has been forced so we went in and looked around. Thirty or forty people would have crowded it. There is a lot of overhead space. By the door there is a stone hollowed out for Holy Water. The church is about 5 feet lower than the surrounding fields. This had all been dug out in the restoration process, and the old burial grounds were visible, but you couldn't tell much about them. Mary Ann climbed up on a mound to take a picture, and a dog tethered up in someone's yard about 15 feet away started saying "What the hell?" Everything is quite close in a walled town.

We walked down the street to the other gate. On the way we saw a second church. It had a new roof, and considerable work had been done on it. You could see where the walls had been repaired, but they were doing a good job. There were 30 or 40 large, numbered pieces of marble lying on the floor. It was a larger structure than the old church. Perhaps 200 people could get into it, with plenty of head space (30 feet). Then we went outside and examined the old gate. It had

Stone wall, Nin

been painted, and had received some minor repairs, and boasted a large inscription saying that it had been repaired in 1969 or whenever.

There is a big, salt evaporation plant on the flat which was formerly covered with water, just outside the wall. I think it is now dry, or half-dry.

We decided to walk around the outside on the edge of the water. There was from 6-15 feet of shore between the old wall and the sea. There were rocks about the size of your fist, some up to the size of a football. (Also lots of rubbish: old shoes, tin cans, etc. I didn't think it was unpleasant, most of it having received the sea treatment.) We would see out into the protected harbor. We walked about ¼ to ½ mile along the old wall. Ivan showed us the sand bar where they swim. They go in a boat. The harbor is well-protected by this sand bar. He showed us some darker areas which are believed to be old Roman breakwaters.

Then we went into the current graveyard, through a breach in the wall, and over the wall of the graveyard. We saw the grave of Zlata's father, and other members of her family. It was the most important mausoleum in the churchyard. There were some people fixing another grave, workmen. We went back through our break in the city wall, out onto the beach again. There were 3 or 4 watch towers on the wall, all in pretty bad states of disrepair. We rounded the circle and came on a man walking a big rowboat. It had a flat bottom, for use in the harbor. There aren't many places along the coast where you can use a flat-bottom boat. Then we turned back into town, through some very narrow streets. The houses are all very old, and the street was 12 feet wide, and the sun was bright. Some of the streets were paved recently, following a visit by Tito, in honor of the 400th or the 800th anniversary of something that happened there. When Tito visits a town, the town gives him presents (a dish, or a gold watch or something), and he gives them presents (15 miles of paving or a town hall or something). He likes it. They like it.

Then we saw the excavation of the Roman temple to Diana. It was very impressive. There is not much above the ground, but there are enough columns and pieces of the frieze lying around that you can see what it was like. They have left the main outlines uncovered. The temple interior was not too big, about the size of our living room at home. The porch was larger, but not much and there had been columns around 3 sides. The columns were 4 feet (in diameter) at the base. We later saw a model in the museum. So we threaded our way around for a couple of hours, less than 100 feet from Diana's temple, to Zlata's mother's house for dinner.

It was a banquet. We had seven courses. First was some ham, *prsat* (pressed). Then fish soup with rice. Then a very nice fish, round with only a big backbone. Then there were *ligmia* (sink fish) prepared two different ways: fried in some butter, and grilled over an open flame. They are a lot

The bridge into Nin

like fried clams, although they prepare them with sea salt. Then there was salad, and finally, some scampi prepared by Zlata's sister-in-law (a good-looking woman of around 30 with a 2-year-old girl and a 5-year-old boy running around). The scampi were very good, and there was a fancy sauce. Finally, there was cheesecake. Eight of us sat around and talked about the family pictures on the wall, how the food was prepared, and things like that. There was wine, made by Zlata's mother from their own grapes. She said that some people around stretch their grape supply by adding sugar when they make wine, but she only uses grapes.

We finished dinner about 3:30 or 4:00. Then Ivan wanted us to see the church. It is St. Aslo's or something like that, and it has the main bell tower in Nin. I was beginning to worry about our hotel reservations in Split (3 or 4 hours away). But we walked half a block to the cathedral. I stopped and traded my sweater for my suit coat at the car, and Ljljana, Zlata's niece, whom we know from Zagreb, laughed at me. They fetched the priest and he came. While they were repairing the tower 2 or 3 years ago, they discovered that it was Roman, possibly a watch tower, and stripped the plaster off, revealing a very handsome white stone structure. The interior of the church is nice — It seems like it is in a little disrepair, but there are some very nice things. A picture on the ceiling has the only really complete picture of a peasant dress from the 15th century. The priest explained everything to us, and Ivan translated. Then he showed us the treasury. He had to open a very big box. We saw a really fine reliquary, containing some portion of St. Aslo, a bishop from the 8th century. It was silver overlaid with gold with four fingers, Christ above, St. Aslo in the middle, and two other saints on the side. You could tell what these men looked like. Beautiful. There was a famous copy of the original, from the 10th century. Also there was a silver coin in a small silver and glass show box, with an arm sticking up, formerly holding the coin. Tradition has it that this is one of the thirty pieces of silver. There is no doubt that it is exactly a coin of that period, but our guide the priest did not want to make any extravagant claims. The only other candidate (for being one of the 30 pieces) is in the Vatican.

We went back out into the sunshine, said goodbye. Then we went to the archeological museum. I was really beginning to be scared about missing our reservation in Split. The museum was small and nice. Ljljana was excited. She worked on the digs last summer, and will work again next summer. She stays with her grandmother, and it is pleasant for her. She was studying mathematics, but doesn't like it very well. She got sick, probably from that, so she left Zagreb and went home to Zadar.

In the museum there were a lot of pins used to hold togas, a gold coin and a silver coin, a very nice Venus, a little shorter than I am, and lots of other little stuff. There were three small rooms. It is exactly next door to

The city of Split, Croatia

Zlata's mother's house. The courtyard on which the two buildings face is called King's Square.

So we had to go. I could have stayed a week, or a month, or all summer. We said good-bye to everyone, and off down the road to Split.

The road from Zadar to Split doesn't touch the coast in so many places, but there are some towns: Sibenick, Premosten, Trogir. And there are some big rivers, like Krk. It's fun to drive along there, and occasionally you get down and drive along the water for a mile or two. Here, when you drive along the water, you REALLY DO DRIVE ALONG THE WATER. The waves lap against the short embankment on which the road is built.

We got to Split about 7:30. Everything was familiar from our visit there in the fall, so I drove straight to the center of town, the dock in front of Diocletian's Palace, and then to our hotel, The Park. I went in, a little apprehensive, and they still had our rooms. So we went up and phoned Xenia, our other Zagreb friend, who goes to Split every two weeks to teach in the university (Descriptive Geometry). She grew up in Split, and her father lives there now. She is the wife of Kreso, who is one of the two who are responsible for me. We had arranged to go to Brac, where they go in the summer, the next day. Xenia came and we had a Coke in the hotel, and talked about our trip. Then I drove Xenia home, and came back and went to bed.

Several Days Later

We got up early and went down to breakfast, so we would be on time for the boat to Brac. We were to be at the boat at 7:30, which we were, and leave at 8:00, which they didn't. We hopped on the boat, a rather large ferry, and, since Xenia and her father were old hands, they knew where the best seats were. It was a very bright, sunshiny, breezy May day (actually April 31, but close). It was clear, and we could see Brac in the distance, 5 or 10 miles away. A lot of people kept getting on the boat, a steady stream. After a while all the seats were taken, and if you got up for a second, someone would grab your seat. The boat left at a quarter to 9, and everyone was feeling pretty good. I think we were the only non-Yugoslavians. The boat made two stops before we got off, Sutevan and Supetar (St. John and St. Peter). They are little towns, clinging to the hillside, with a church, a hotel and 100 or so houses. Rather attractive, Mediterranean, quiet. About half of the passengers got off at Supetar, and climbed into a waiting bus, to go to the other side of the island. There are pines on the island, the water is beautifully clear and blue, but the beaches are pebbles and rocks, not sand. The island is covered with pines, short and not of timber quality. There are some fields. We saw some that were terraced with stone walls on the sides and through them, in an attempt to keep the soil. There is a road along the shore, and there are cars, but relatively few.

So we got off at Splitska. It is the location of the quarries which supplied the stone for Diocletian's Palace. It is smaller than the other two towns, consisting of two old, big, fortified houses and a new market-butcher shop. The old houses were built by Xenia's ancestors, some of them. They emigrated from England at the time of Bloody Mary, and went to Venice, and then to Brac. The house was fortified against attacks by the Moorish pirates, who lived several miles down the coast, on the mainland at the mouth of a river.

We went to Xenia's father's house, a summer home, which was less than a quarter of a mile from the dock. The house is divided in two now, having been built by Xenia's grandfather, probably after the First World War. There was about ½ acre of land, which had all been a flower garden. Now there are jasmine, lilacs and other flowering shrubs, all old and rather overgrown. Quite a few trees, an olive, etc. They have a very nice terrace with a view across the water, and are only a few feet farther away from the edge than you are, although the main highway passes between the terrace and the sea. The main highway has cars about once every ½ hour, but in the European spirit, slamming along.

We sat in the sunshine, rather welcome because the breeze was fresh. And after a while we had lunch. Bread and cheese and baloney. They carried it in their bags for us. It tasted very good. I was promoting the swimming, in an exploratory way, because it wasn't a clear case.

After lunch we walked up the road, and met some of Xenia's cousins, who were working on their boats. We saw the chapel where her mother is buried, and walked down the road toward Prosterina, the town where the boat waits until it is time to go back. We went down the road a mile or two. There were several houses being built, and one really expensive house which was new, and enclosed in a fence. The house of a Party Official.

Then we walked back. Xenia said she would show me the best place to go swimming. Each wind is associated with a place to swim. So we went off in the other direction, down the road. There had been a band playing off an on, down by the dock, in honor of the holiday. As we went by the fortified house, now the restaurant, we could see the band eating their dinner. They were also drinking lots of wine.

As we walked along a lady called to Xenia to come and see her new house. She was a retired school teacher, who had taught in Splitska, and had borrowed money to build a house, which she hoped to be able to rent in the summer season. Mary Ann went and looked at it. It was quite modern and had an American bathroom, a nice terrace, etc.

So we walked on, and the boys, Patrick, Danny and Davor went on ahead. We could see them across the inlet, ½ mile away. But they didn't look like they were swimming much. We finally got over to where they were, after a little scrambling off the road through the pines. I decided to go in, and after slipping off into the trees to change, and the usual slow torture getting in, it was really nice. About like Corporation Beach when I am there. So I swam off down the shore, in the lovely clear water, and after a while I decided to go out and walk back. A big mistake, as the rocks were really sharp. So I went into the trees and tried to get back on the pine straw.

After a while I did. People were beginning to wonder would the restaurant close on us? So I suggested that they go ahead and I would catch up.

So I walked home in the sunshine, and caught up with them about halfway. Then we went to the restaurant and had dinner in a private room, just the right size for the eight of us. It was very good: roast lamb, cooked out over a spit, potatoes, salad, soup and a bottle of Brac wine. Tremendous.

Then we went back. Xenia's father took a nap, and I sat in the sunshine.

The boat came at 6:00 and we were there waiting. We went inside and got good seats, and rode back to Split, getting there at 8:00. We said goodbye on the dock, and went home to our hotel and after a little while went to bed.

The next morning we got up a little later. We had decided to go see Trogir. We went downstairs and had breakfast. I tried to get an American breakfast, but they didn't really want to give it to me, so I ended up with a lonely little fried egg, which tasted pretty good even so.

So we went out to the car and off down the road to Trogir, another old town about 15 miles up the coast. It was the holiday, not too much traffic, people acting a little as if they didn't know what to do.

Trogir is a walled city, on an island, not very big, say, compared to Split. When we got there we crossed the bridge, 30 or 40 feet in length, and after ¼ miles we were on the pier next to an old fort by a Parking sign. So we parked and walked around the fort, which was all closed up, and across the soccer field, and so we decided we had better walk downtown. We walked down the pier, which was stone, and 20 or 30 feet deep alongside, and after a little came to a gate in the wall by an ice cream wagon. We went in. By now one of these medieval cities doesn't surprise me the way they first did, but even so, it was nice. We went in an old church, and then walked down to the main square. There were a few people around, a busload of high school kids came out of the cathedral. The square isn't too big — About as wide as it is from your house to the garage. The cathedral is not huge, but it has an elegant door, carved by a Florentine, but in a Croatian spirit. Not completely religious.

The inside has one tomb with half a dozen statues, such as St. John, an early bishop who perhaps founded this church. We went in and saw the church treasury. There were nice things, but it was not the same as at Nin, lacking the personalized treatment. They were selling postcards and other things in the treasury. But there was no denying the beauty and the value of the display: the gold cups, statues, bishops' miters and vestments, etc.

So there we went out, and the boys were agitating — enough rubbernecking. But we walked into the town, where every street is an alley, and they give out unexpectedly. Subiceva is a big thoroughfare in Zagreb near our house, but it is a 10 foot wide alley in Trogir (the Subic hometown).

So we wandered back to the gate and bought some ice cream from the nice little girl tending the stand. Then we parked the boys on a bench while I went back to ask the lady in the Tourist place where I could go swimming. She said I could go anywhere I wanted to, after a slight pause to recover from the shock of the idea. Actually she was a little nicer than that, and told me 3 or 4 routes I could take, which I had more or less figured out. Also the statement of the principle, go in where you like, was exactly what I wanted.

So we crossed a second bridge onto the island of Ciovo. We drove

Ciovo

along an asphalt road for 3 miles, when it gave out, and then continued along a dirt road. There were moments when it wasn't clear that it was a road, but then we'd see a sign for a bus stop, or something. We could always see the edge of the water, but never just the right place. But then we saw it in the distance. An old stone ruin of a fortified house, right on the edge of the water. It was about ½ mile from the road, and we climbed down a very small valley, as opposed to the completely rocky hillsides on either side. The little valley was the reason the house had been there in the first place. Someone had planted grapes and things there now, but there were no houses anywhere around. When we got to the bottom there were two picnic groups that had come in boats. But there was a lot of room, and I changed and went in the water. It was very painful on my feet, even worse than the day before. Also the two or three feet of beach wasn't too clean — Bottles and cans and other flotsam and jetsam. But the water was crystal clear, and very blue out across the bay, where we could see Trogir glinting in the sun. So I swam around for awhile, and came out and got dressed, and Patrick went in and swam,

Trogir

and Danny ducked. Then we climbed back up through the fields, which were filled with wildflowers, a sort of punk daisy, daisies, blue flowers of some sort, and some yellow bushes. We picked some bunches of them, but they weren't too spruce when we got back to our hotel.

So then we drove back to Split to meet Xenia for a tour of Split, and to get those boys fed.

When we got back they were serving on the terrace of our hotel, which is really pretty nice, and not too expensive. So we sat out under the trees and had cheese soufflé (Mary Ann), spaghetti (Danny), raznici (Patrick), fried cheese (me). I lost. And some white wine from Split (very good).

But then we had to hurry to meet Xenia. We went to the Aquarium which was closed, and to the top of the mountain, where we could see Brac, Hvar, Ciovo and the beautiful city of Split. There were two mountaintops, and we had to climb some. By then I was feeling my swim and my ½ litre. But we drove down through the park, past the Hajduk (soccer team) stadium, in front of the old palace, where we parked. We went to see the basement of the palace. It is very impressive architecturally, massive stone arches to support the palace, but not worth 4 dinars, since there wasn't anything else to see, but this big sequence of empty basement rooms, and you could see such a room before going through the gate. That's the way it is being a tourist. Xenia said that when she was there before, they had a stone with Diocletian's wife carved on it.

Taking a tour in Split

So there we said goodbye again, until Zagreb, and went home. We had a very nice dinner, beefsteak, etc., less than $2 a piece for everything. The best hotel in Split.

The next morning we got up very early, 6:00, in order to be able to stop at Andelika's to pick up Joan. We ate breakfast and retraced our steps along the Adriatic. We were at Karlobag, over the Velebit (the name of the ridge) in no time at all. It was not quite so nice as it had been the two preceding nights.

At 1:00 or so we got to the turn off the Prozor, and followed Angelica's directions, and were driving down this one car-wide road when we met a farmer on a wagon. We jockeyed so we could pass, and I asked, "Nu Prozor?" He said, "Da, da, Prozor." So we kept going, came to some very rocky spots, and then there were Joan and Angelica walking on down the road. So we put them in the car, and off to Anjika's house. It was a brick house, in a cluster of 5 or 6 houses. We drove into the yard, and I parked my car.

We went into the house, and Angelica's grandmother was tending the stove. She is 78, but she shows her age more than you do. We met Angelica's sister Jadranka (Joan says that is Adriana), who is 15. So, Angelica said we should have some lunch, sarma, which is ground ham rolled in cabbage leaves and cooked with vinegar. It was very good, having been on the stove all morning waiting for us.

After a while Angelica's father and mother came in from the fields. They had been planting potatoes. He is a very nice man. He said he wished we would stay a week. There were lots of things he wanted to ask us. I tried to talk Croatina, and had some luck but not complete success. It is the first time Angelica can remember that they had so much livestock. It had started to rain. Jadranka and her father pulled the wagon in out of the rain.

They wouldn't let us go without eating again. So we had ham and bread. Joan had a very good time while she was there. He gave me a good bottle of Slivovitz.

So there we drove home. Where we got near Zagreb the traffic was very bad. There was an accident on the road near Jastrabarska. Go 100 yards, stop. It took us more than an hour to go 10 miles. But we got home about 7:00, while it was still light.

Joan calls these my epic letters.

I hope you are OK, and that EA is there and OK, and happier than when she last wrote. Tel her we love her, and to say thank you after she has had something good to eat.

All my love,
Tom

PS Mary Ann is going to make reservations to fly to Boston (we will get to Hyannis) on June 1. –T

MEXICO

MEXICO
Mérida
Cancún
Chichén Itzá
Uxmal

The people of Mexico, in large part, are mixtures of Spanish and Indian genetic heritage. These people are strong.

The biggest challenge for them has come from their neighbors form the North, the United States.

As a tourist, one gets the feeling that considerable energy is spent to raise the standard of living up to ours.

Mexico

THIS WAS WRITTEN AS A LETTER TO MY DAUGHTER ELIZABETH, AND HER THEN-HUSBAND RUSSELL WILLIAMSON, AND MY GRANDSONS, CALEB AND HIRAM. The trip to Mexico took place from August 22-29, 1987.

It was not our first foreign trip since our year in Yugoslavia, but it was the first about which I wrote another epic letter.

We had arranged a tour, to be met in Mérida (on the Yucatán Peninsula), to proceed from there to Cancún, stopping at Chichén Itzá to view the archeological site along the way.

Dear Elizabeth, Rusty, Caleb and Hiram,Aug. 25, 1987

We are now at our hotel near Chichén Itzá. We have walked through the digs, and it began to rain just as we were finishing. I climbed the pyramid here, and the pyramid at Uxmal yesterday, and came down on the chain, both times, although younger and more confident people did not clutch the chain. I am beginning to get into the climbing around on pyramids.

Our trip has been interesting, and more or less scheduled, but very little goes exactly as scheduled around here. To begin with, our flight was cancelled. So we had to decide – did we want to wait in Atlanta until Sunday, or fly to Mexico City and spend the night there? We chose Mexico, so they took our ticket, and gave us some mimeographed form to replace it. No one beyond the airport girl who gave it to us had ever seen these forms before, and at each stage it had to be passed up to higher and higher officials for verification (at least to the manager of the airport, etc.).

We stayed overnight at the Holiday Inn by the airport, The high point of our stay here was listening to 3 girls play the guitar and sing in the bar while I had my first XX (Dos Equis). They weren't great singers, but they were alive, I guess. In the morning, we were taken to the airport to catch a Mexicana (as opposed to Air Mexico), and we waited around for 1&1/2 hours, time well spent, while the officials pondered our mimeographed page which was now our ticket. When the plane flew they gave us breakfast, which included sweet potato casserole, a hard-boiled egg and baloney and a cookie. We saw two coasts of the Gulf of Mexico, the one as we flew over Mérida, and 1 jillion miles of undeveloped sand beach.

Our tour included the taxi to town, so we were put into a VW bus, and the driver was given our voucher. Then, it turns out, that on Sunday the street our hotel was on is closed to vehicles so people can walk down it, so our poor cab driver could not deliver us, nor tell us why he could not. But I figured it out, grabbed our suitcases and walked about 50 yards to the front door of the Mérida Mission, much to the relief of the cab driver, who could not abandon his cab.

On Sunday we walked to the market in Mérida. Mérida is 200,000+ people and many people walk to the market, and go to the movie ("Crocodile Dundee"), etc. About 1 block from our hotel there is a small park attached to a church, with a statue honoring maternity. It is a mistake. That's all they do here — really. Needless to say we bought some things. The market is wild. You can get tortillas anywhere, but the Mexicans only buy them at one place, where they are being baked while you watch. But we didn't eat anything. We came back and went to the outdoor bar, and it started to pour cats and dogs, and I had XX, and XX and some *hors d'ouvres* for $7, your mother, too. We looked out over the patio. Through the downpour. Then it stopped raining and we went to dinner at a very nice restaurant that was not very expensive. I had lime soup, which was very good, and red snapper cooked in butter, which was

OK, a very good margarita, etc. Then we sat in the playa and watched the citizens in all phases of the maternity project, from young children, oblivious — to elderlies, presumably oblivious, with 5+ gradations in between.

August 26

The next morning we went to Uxmal. The tourism industry here is in a primitive stage, and it is getting organized slowly. I think 3rd worlders are sharing tourism technology. There are non-trivial parallels with Yugoslavia. The guides go to school, and they must take tests, etc. We got shifted from our bus driver to another bus driver to be our guide through the digs. The guide we had was pretty good, but he recited memorized pages, and did not like questions. There is a very nice long decorated building in Uxmal. The archway has a very pleasant breeze going through it all of the time. Maybe that's why they located it the way they did. They have, say 25+ people trying to keep the jungle back, and they are losing in a major way. The pyramid is fun. You can step out of the mouth of the god and survey 500+ tourists down below.

Uxmal, Mexico

After we had done Uxmal in good shape (for example there is a very nice ball park which looks up at the earlier-mentioned arch, which poses a very interesting question—how did they play it?), we went to Kabah, which for practical purposes has not been touched, except to put a road over one of the main buildings, actually only a small corner of it. Our stay there lasted 15+/- minutes, and our guide cut us off from a non-trivial portion of the town, so he could get home a little earlier. Then we went to a hotel which has a very nice view of the pyramid at Uxmal from the lobby, which was 3+/- miles away. Our meal was part of the package we bought, and I had chicken, Yucatán-style, rice, and a fried banana (the first time I had that, I think). That was the best thing from that meal. We rushed a little, so we could go swimming. There was a very pleasant pool, with a view in one corner, of the pyramid. You had to work to get a tree out of the way.

Then, after our pleasant swim, we hopped into our VW bus. The two other passengers were a Mexican and his wife, aged 50+/-, who, on the way to Uxmal, sat in front of us, and were billing and cooing, not too offensively, but it was a puzzle. He wanted to talk about various subjects with us, such as how clean the streets are in Mérida (true +/-, except for millions of discarded corncobs) but I let your mother field that one.

That night we went out on our own, and found a true second-class restaurant, where I got the most expensive thing on the menu, "filet mignon," for $4+/-. This differed from the "minute steak" by having a piece of bacon wrapped around it, but there was still quite a bit of meat there. The worst part of the meal was that we arrived late and our table was only half in the pleasant dining area, and a trifle near the kitchen. Your mother ordered Yucatan pork roast, and they brought Yucatan broiled fish, which is not completely easy to identify, since it has a tomato and several other vegetables like carrots and some white carrot types all over it, so she started to eat it, and gave me a bite and said, "Does that taste like pork to you?" The waiter grabbed her dish, and said, "You ordered pork" and slapped the Yucatan pork in its place. I am certain that

Pyramid at Uxmal

he made only minor repairs to the fish and took it to its proper owner. While all this went on I had XX and XX and managed to get filled.

Then, on the advice of our *Fodor's* Guide, which up to this point had been uniformly incorrect (wrong addresses, wrong names, etc.), we went to see some regional folk dancing, sponsored by some government entity, that was held up the street. We had to stand, pressed up against a bunch of paisanos. There were 300+ spectators, and 20+/- dancers , and a brass band, and they performed 8 regional dances, some of which evolved from minuets, climaxed by (1) an XX bottle on the head by a girl and a boy, and (2) an XX bottle and 4 glasses of water on a tray, on the heads and (3) as above, standing on rather small boxes, acting somewhat like drums. They weren't so sensational as the Yugoslav bottle on the head types but perhaps I have lived too long. At any rate there were paisanos behind me who whistled in good shape. The dancers were very good, and later knowledge suggests that they are a farm team for the big league, which is the Folklórico in Cancún, which performs every night. One boy fell down during the last dance, but really that was the only mis-step I saw. To the hotel, to bed.

August 27

On Wednesday morning we ate breakfast in our hotel (fresh orange juice, scrambled eggs, my best breakfast). We then shaped up in the lobby so we could wait around for our transportation. So we looked in the hotel gift shop. Almost every single place we have looked at has exactly the same things for exactly the same price. The persons attending are on a commission. We brought some stuff (naturally) and the lady was very sweet, the first person in Mexico who acted as if we were real people, doing something (buying presents for our grandchildren). Not that we talked to her very much.

Then our transportation to Chichén Itzá arrived, a full-sized Dodge, 70+/-, AC, without all of the Freon. Our guide was quite voluble with our Mexican co-tourists, and was capable of communication with us, but nothing complicated. The road from Mérida to Chichén Itzá was very good, with a paved shoulder, the only good road we drove on.

Riding with us, in the Dodge, was a very interesting man, whose first question was, did I like Mexican art? He said he had long been interested in the Mexican Impressionists, and had known a man who was sub-director of the Museum of Modern Art for more than 25 years. He took all of his vacations in Mexico, but he hadn't been to the digs before. He had just purchased a sculpture from his friend, which he had been trying to get for a long time, 15 years. Art was his preoccupation. We walked through the digs with him, but it was warm and quite humid, and it rained on us a little, and he didn't like that very much. I climbed the pyramid, and made the circle tour at the top, looking in each of the cardinal directions. I was a little apprehensive at the top — someone of the 10+/- people milling around might make an unexpected move – but it didn't bother me very much. The sense of depth and volume from there is very strong – the pyramid below you – the Temple of the Warriors and the hundred or so columns by its side, and the large numbers of birds swooping and soaring in the intervening space, provided an experience that can be recycled, perhaps to make me feel good some time. I suppose that is the point of seeing different places. On my descent I came down, holding the chain loosely for moral support, but much more confident than on Uxmal. The next time I could came down without it. There was a lady who had come up 30 or so steps, and was very frightened. But she had her purse, and a non-trivial carry-on bag, which to my mind was interfering with her balance. At any rate she turned around and went back. I learned later that this not uncommon – two or three of the assorted people we met had done this.

Temple of the Warriors, Chichén Itzá

Then we saw the Temple of the Warriors, which is Toltec, although Chac Mool lives at the top. Your mother climbed the stairs, 30+/-, and we wandered around the platform. She didn't like going down the stairs much. The risers are 4-6 inches, and it would be a 30-foot fall, but it is easy to go down sideways. Then we went back to the entrance, souvenir area, were met by our transportation, who took is to the outdoor dinner. These seem to be well-organized by the tourist industry.

We stayed at the hotel, which had the ambience of a hacienda, with tile floors, a brick roof, and windows with shutters which open on the courtyard. There is an air-conditioner designed to blow a cool breeze through the room, and massive hacienda furniture. There is a little park next to the motel with a small zoo: monkey, several birds and small bunch of deer. In addition I saw a little bird which I tentatively identify as a *banana quit*, because he was going "quit-quit-quit" in a banana tree. We had a nap, and swam (in the pool at the same time as our German co-tour takers, 3 rotund prosperous-appearing men, who engaged in earnest conversation all of the time, even while splashing in the pool). There was a tour consisting of French speakers, 16+/-. Later information causes me to suspect that they were from Quebec.

That night we took a taxi to the light show, which is centered on the pyramid at Chichén Itzá, and the other buildings are lit up intermittently during the show. They can make the pyramid several colors – to me the most effective is green for the main mass, and red for the temple on the top, the red lights coming from inside. When I was up there I saw the light installation. I think it is a good thing — the installations don't leave any mark and tourism is now the #2 industry in Mexico. We played the game for getting seats very well, getting two on the first row. About 4 minutes into the show, we got a nice little shower, which lasted 5+/- minutes, and we retired to a spot under a tree, and lost our seats. There were some college kids providing the sound, and it was not pitched at my level, and added little to my rapidly-growing body of information about the Maya. The best thing was their explanation of the snake — it goes like this:

The snake was supposed to provide the rain. The rainy season begins in the spring. At the solstice there is a shadow created on the balustrade along the stairs up the pyramid. At the bottom the snake's head is about 8 feet long.

The light show version is not calendar dependent, but since we had 3 or 4 showers during our visit, one may presume that it was equally effective.

Our taxi waited for us during the show. The driver seemed to be 18+/- years old, was very nicely dressed, and charged us $4 for the round trip. He was upset that one of the dollars which I paid him had a corner missing, a tiny corner, but fortunately your mother had a whole bill. Our trip was 2 kilometers +/- each way, just barely too far to walk.

August 28

The next morning we had breakfast at our motel, then back to the digs. This time we went by ourselves. It was fun to be able to take our time,

Mayan construction

and to go slowly over the things we had been shown the preceding afternoon. I spent about ¾ hr. in the ball park, trying to figure it all out. How could the game have been played? It is not clear. There seems to be one written account, by the Bishop Landa. To me he does not seem too reliable — since his whole report is the justification of unbelievable barbarity by the Spaniards in order to get the Indians to abandon the practice of human sacrifice. Then I climbed some stairs up to a small room overlooking the ball park. There was a guard there. There was a wooden lintel, made of sapote, carved by the Maya. It was 2 ft. X 18 ft., I suppose, and it supported 5 tons of rock. But the Mayans knew what they were doing — the stones were so carefully fitted that the lintel itself probably did not carry more than 1/5 of the weight. On the outside there were tigers drawn on some of the stones. Then we looked at the platform of the skulls, and your mother sat on a nice jaguar, and we slowly worked our way to the place where there are "1000 columns." They are 7 feet tall, about 12 feet apart, and there must have been a roof. There was a path leading out the back, rather narrow and untended, so we went by ourselves down the path. There are massive piles of rubble on the left side, pure unadulterated jungle on the right. After going say 150 feet along the path we climbed a little rise, say 25 feet high, and when we got to the top, we saw another bunch of columns, 100+/-, just the same as the ones left behind, but fairly far along in the process of being swallowed by the jungle. From the rise, off to the right, we could see some other buildings. We got our site map, and after some study decided they were the "market" and a "bath." The map shows several practice fields for the ball game, but they are totally jungleized, and you must have to whack through with a machete to find the goal line. Aspects of this game have been pondered and scrutinized by historians and anthropologists for centuries.

By this time it was probably getting to be 11 o'clock, and your mother was beginning to show signs that she had had enough sun, and so had I. It is simply hotter at that latitude.

So we went to the souvenir place, and I bought two volumes by Stephens, *Incidents of Travel in Yucatán*. This is indeed a great book. Then we looked at the stuff that was too expensive, had a Coke and took the taxi to our hotel. We went swimming for 20 or 30 minutes. It was approximately 1 o'clock, since that was check-out time, and I asked the desk clerk for dispensation. He went away and came back after a while and said it was all right. This seems to be the drill.

Anyway, the swimming was great. My new book informed me that swimming in the "cenote" was a standard part of Stephens' routine during his stay in 1842, from 1 o'clock to 2 o'clock. They insisted that the women go somewhere else when they swam. We saw that very cenote during both of our walks through the digs. The first time it looked uninviting, green with algae, almost the color and consistency of pea soup. But in the morning it was calm, the algae had all collected on one side and it looked inviting, not worse than the abandoned strip mine I learned to swim in when I was a boy.

We skipped lunch, snoozed, and prepared to be met by a bus at 3:00. The bus came about 2:30, and disgorged 30+/- people. While we waited for the bus, your mother talked to a lady who was associated with a different tour agency from the one we had, and there was no indication when she was supposed to be picked up. When she asked to use the phone she learned — there is no phone in the hotel. We asked to buy stamps — there are no stamps closer to Chichén Itzá than Mérida or Cancún.

We finally were allowed on the bus at 4:10. The lady in charge of the tour first told us that we would have to split up, then she spotted the two empty seats. So we got on the bus for a very bumpy ride through the tropics. There were a few villages. The people all live in huts, thatched with palm. Sometimes you can see in. There is no furniture, a dirt floor, and the people sleep in hammocks, cook in the yard, and there are no outhouses, or electricity. One or two people in a village may have a dilapidated automobile. There are no schools. We stopped to buy souvenirs at the town of Vallodolid. It is supposed to be a good town, but there is no evidence of this along the road we were on. I don't know what I expected, but this is much worse.

The ride to Cancún lasted 3½ hours, and it was dusk when we

arrived. We drove through the support town. There are hotels there, presumably less expensive, but not much, than the one we booked.

When our bus brought us to our hotel we checked into our room, and it was very nice. It was on the main floor, had a TV which did not work.

Then we went to dinner in our hotel. The restaurant was adjacent to the pool, half outdoors, and had pretensions. There was a band, playing modern jazz with a slight Mexican flavor (the leader would get out a basketball size gourd and shake it around now and then, ordinarily he played a flute). The only song I recognized was "Laura," but it was pleasant, though a little loud since it was designed to stretch out onto the beach, that is, the electronic enhancer was so turned.

We went to bed after one set, say 9:45.

August 29

The next morning we had breakfast, and then went down to the beach. We were in the water an hour or so, and then came out and sat under a large palm thatched umbrella for two or three hours. I went into the hotel, in the hall downstairs, where the tourist agency representatives were posted, at tables. My representative was a soccer player, waiting for the siesta so he could go practice. I arranged for a snorkel trip, and the dinner at the Folklórico. He made reservations which I was to pick up in the late afternoon. The cost was $50 for each outing, for both of us.

Then we had lunch in the big bar/lunch facility on the beach. Then we went to our rooms and slept and read until time for the Folklo'rica.

The dinner theater was in the municipal building, a convention center, a little more than half a mile from the hotel. We took a taxi, and arrived 20 minutes early (to my dismay), but it was alright, since then we had first choice of tables. We were served one drink, a tequila sunrise, I suppose, and then went through the serving line. It was OK, but the enchiladas could have been omitted, the sauce ran into everything, and I like the style at home with sour cream all over everything better. As we finished, the musicians started. There were perhaps 6 in all, and their purpose was to play every instrument ever invented, rather than play well. There was a man who played the pipes of Pan, which I had never heard before. When I said this to the lady across the table from me, she turned to look, but then her husband said he had never even seen anything like that before, let alone heard it. They were from Nashville, and this was their 4th trip to Mexico, and he had bought time-sharing in a condo 5 years ago. They had their daughter, aged 6, with them, and had rented a car.

After a while the dancers began the program. There were 12 different dancers, I suppose, beginning with a Mayan dance (modern dance with Mayan costumes). Each dance had its own costume and stage backdrop. I liked them all – the rope twirler as much as any, I suppose – although the girls dancing with lit candles on their heads, white dresses, and the lights turned down was nice.

Then we walked back to our hotel, the lagoon on the right, whizzing cars on our left. It took about 20 minutes to walk back. I had to pause once for a minute or two to get my bearings, but in fact we did not take any false steps, which was pretty good, since the convention center is circular, the various roads leading out are similar in appearance, etc.

August 30

Friday morning, after breakfast, we reported to the marina of a nearby hotel for our snorkel trip. After waiting around for ½-¾ hour for the other 4 snorklers, who were from Montreal and 2 only spoke French, we got onto a 20-foot boat with an outboard motor. The guide was a very nice guy, who had not long been at it, and his assistant was a boy, who did

Swimming in Mexico

not speak English. The boat had a glass bottom. Before long we saw some interesting coral, and I was ready to jump out, but our guide was not enthusiastic. So we went on for 5 minutes or so, and he put us down near a boat tending scuba divers. The waves were a little choppy, say 2 feet, but with professional flippers you are quite mobile. I started out a wrong way, and the bottom was mostly sand, with a little grass or something. But then I worked my way back to the reef, which was on the other side of the boat. This was definitely more interesting. There were large schools of little (3-5 inch) fish, non-descript, yellowish, and above them 2 or 3 bright yellow fish (8 to 10 inches). I don't know if they are related. There were some very bright green fish, with a black stripe through the middle (6 inches), and 30 or 40 light grey with black trim gathered underneath the boat. There were somewhat small for grouper, grouper-like fish on the outskirts looking on. There were some brain coral and some bush-like coral. The bush-like coral seemed to prefer 10-12 feet of water. So after 20 minutes or so, we took off for the Isla Mujeres. We anchored just outside an area which was provided for novice snorklers. There were about 40 of them in there, learning to adjust their masks, running into each other, seeing a minnow now and then, etc. I decided to save my energy, but I should have sent Mary Ann in. We waited there about 1 hour. The French Canadians didn't appear on schedule, and the tour guide tried to blow on a conch shell to summon them back. But he didn't know how. So I showed him how (make your lips vibrate). A great triumph.

So after a while we motored to our pre-arranged dinner, another buffet. Then we went to the town, in case we wanted to buy souvenirs, silver, gold, black coral or plastic. There was one nice air-conditioned shop. But I was impatient to get back to snorkeling. After the F.C.'s took an interminable time to finish their shopping we started for home. This time we anchored near a rock which was about 15 feet above the water, the size of a small house. There was a current, say 4 M.P.H., around the rock. It was a good snorkeling spot. When I first went in I went down current at first, but the guide's helper intercepted me, and turned me around. I had probably gone 100 feet in 3 or 4 minutes. So then I worked my way back, up current from the boat. It was not an awful lot different from the morning snorkeling, but I did see some barracuda, which camouflaged themselves nicely against the coral, appearing at first glance to be one of the branches.

Their general appearance is quite different from those at Nassau, being smaller and more snakelike. They also have a design on their backs, like a snake. So maybe they were eels.

I saw one lovely bright-orange fish. The guide said it might be a red snapper. It was the right size to be one. The rock itself was interesting — there were lots of different-sized holes in it — I looked in one the size of a quarter and a little fish poked his head out at me, and then pulled it back in. Only one side of the rock had coral, the other was much less interesting, being mainly limestone.

The tourist industry had placed a small statue, a Mary I suppose, about two feet below the surface in a niche on the rock. So it was something to see.

After swimming for about ¾ hour, I figured I had seen it, and went back to the boat. I was beginning to be a little tired, and took off my flippers before climbing the ladder.

On the way back to Cancún I had a couple of margaritas. The trip was advertised as "Open Bar," and our guide had brought a non-trivial amount of alcohol, more than ½ bottle apiece, plus beer.

It was pleasant riding in a little boat across the lagoon, nursing a margarita as the sun tapered off a little. Although I stayed in the shade all of the time, I knew I had gotten some sunburn from the reflection. Still, it was all in a good cause.

We arrived back at 5:00, our guide had given us an hour extra. We walked back to our hotel, had dinner.

The next morning we caught the plane and headed home.

SPAIN

Spain has a rich history as a country of Europe, from its settlement by Greeks, Romans, Moslems and others. It is not overly prosperous, but it received substantial reward from its new world colonies. The Napoleonic Wars took away a lot of that, and the Spanish Civil War of the 1930s left them reeling. They were fortunate to remain neutral during World War II.

When we were there, a big effort was being devoted to promote tourism.

September 3 (1988)

THE FLIGHT TO MADRID WAS 6 HOURS AND IT WAS EARLY IN THE MORNING. You can see the hills outside Madrid and the arid countryside.

There was a 1-hour flight to Barcelona. Most of the people got off at Madrid, and the plane was cleaned while we were in the airport. Not that clean. The stewardesses who stayed on were relaxed, glad that the trip was over. It is a lot of work serving a full plane two meals and cocktails, etc.

We got off the plane at Barcelona, after flying over the coast for a few minutes. It took 10-15 minutes to pick up our luggage, then we walked out and there was a hotel-reservation kiosk right there. The young lady booked us here, the Hotel Catalunya, which is Catalonian for "Catalonia." We asked her how to get to the train, which we got to on the moving sidewalk. Before that I changed $100, which took much too long. On the other hand, it was lucky I did, since the banks closed at noon until Monday morning. We got off the train and walked to the Metro in good shape. It was mildly confusing finding our hotel, carrying suitcases, but we got there, at approximately noon, a few minutes before check-out time.

We went to our room, and the beds were not made up. We went out and walked down the Ramblas and looked at the businesses. Then we went into the Plaza Real, an old plaza which we soon learned was a popular hang-out for pot dealers. It was a pleasant, enclosed, old square. We had our lunch of large shrimp cooked in olive oil and I had a large glass of beer. The large shrimp were $1 a piece, but things here are not inexpensive. After ¾ hour we continued our stroll down to the waterfront, where we saw the Columbus monument. At the second level we located 2 Pinsons (not 1 but 2). One's name is Martín — Which seems to be one of the most common Catalonian names.

Then we walked down and decided not to board Columbus' ship, the *Santa Maria*. It's not very large — about 40 feet long, and it had a couple of small cannons.

The sunshine was very warm, and we decided to try to locate the Picasso Museum. The emphasis at this point is try, because we managed to have an extensive tour of Barcelona. The problem was map reading. We have a detailed street map, which we consulted frequently, but street names change every block or two. And the street signs frequently refer only to the corner, or something else. I don't dislike wandering around the streets of an old town. Eventually we found Princessa St., which we had passed much earlier, and then the tiny street, Montcada, which is no more than an alley but looked like a real street on the map.

We went down the little street, about 50 feet, and there was the museum. You enter, and find yourself in a beautiful courtyard. There is a man giving tickets, which are free. To get to the museum you must climb some stairs, up one flight, and off to the side there are two rooms of ceramics, donated by Francoise, Picasso's wife. They are elegant, and I suppose, representative. Some faces, birds...perhaps 75 pieces. Lots of jugs.

The proper exhibit began with sketch books from 1894-95+, and studies of body parts, etc., from the time that Picasso was a teenager. There were some fine portraits of his father and mother and other relatives, those he could get to pose. There were numerous landscapes – Difficult to paint, but representational. He solved in a very effective way the problem of distribution of masses, without wasting paint. The major work displayed from the period (when he was 16-18-years-old), was a sick bed scene, with a woman in bed, a doctor, a mother perhaps, seated in a chair. It was 8 feet x 5 feet (+), and there was a window in the picture.

At this stage there were several portraits: friends, I suppose, and a fine portrait of his father. The next major set of pictures was from the Blue Period. There was a very lovely portrait of a girl, and another of the same girl with a very bleak look on her face — Almost ageless in the 2nd picture. There were 15 or so blues — One major one with a man embracing his wife, and she has a red apron — It must be a grief picture. The same room has a horse, in a death agony, some disproportion, dated 1917, clearly the embryo of "Guernica."

Then there was a 15-year jump in time, to some cubist paintings. There was a portrait and a still life, but not very many pictures from this period. There are some large rooms in the museum that are not yet fixed up for displaying painting. It looks as if they are taking their time, and doing it right.

There are two rooms devoted to Picasso's study of Velasquez's great painting – called here "The Mennines." The two rooms are a beautiful lecture in how to think about modern art. The paintings consist of very detailed steps in arriving at the final form of Picasso's interpretation of the Infanta, and the girl with the teacup, but Picasso was not much interested in the dwarf, which is almost the dominating figure in Velasquez's original. In the second room, there are 3 versions of the whole scene, about 4 ft. x 5 ft. They are not exactly the same size. The one on the right is mostly black, or has a lot of black. The other two use all of the colors of the set. Picasso loved the painter, and in some ways the picture says, "That's the way it looks to me." He's back there looking through a key hole.

Those 3 pictures side by side are incredible. I can understand why

Picasso didn't let them out — Who was Picasso to be making a comment on "the greatest painting in the world"? But now, people can come and see who he was – he has left all of the evidence — and you can hear these two giants talking to each other, across the centuries. Being in those two rooms was an incredible experience, worth the trip to Europe — Picasso is simply telling you — Enjoy yourself — But he isn't just a hedonist. — He was not disrespectful to religion, or any ideas that other people cling to fervently...except the right to make war.

The next room has the bullfight engravings and the copper plates — There must be 30 of them. They are impressive as they are displayed — A symphony of distribution of black and white, the whole pattern made by all of them as interesting as each one. I don't really like bullfighting, or approve of the activity of analyzing the whole operation to decide whether some move was done well or not. Killing bulls is a logical step in having meat to eat, but, while it is ancient, doing it in a stylized ceremony seems primitive to me.

There is a room with 4 or 5 more pictures of Francoise. You can watch her getting sick of posing, as you go through the sequence. In the first picture she is star-struck, very young looking. Later in the series, you can watch her wonder in her mind why Pablo doesn't want to join the jet set.

The next room had several pictures with faun and the woman.

There was a room with doves (or pigeons) in the windows. The blues and whites and greens in those paintings are beautiful, and his pleasure that the war was over oozes out of them. It was getting dark, and I had too much to think about.

We walked down 3 flights of stairs to the courtyard. It was too late to go in the shop — They had closed. The museum guards were standing there, ready to go home.

By then it was getting very near to supper time, and we had only had beer and shrimp for lunch, so we wandered back to the street of our hotel. We went into a bar/restaurant, and asked if they were ready to serve, and the girl at the front of the bar went back to the kitchen and said yes. The waiter came, and we ordered paella and salad and a bottle of wine. We poured oil and vinegar on our salad. Oil and vinegar are the best here in Spain where they are fresh and not stored.

Then we had the paella, which was great. There was a very large shrimp, several smaller, and a lot of mussels all of the way through the rice. It had a very delicate, fresh sea taste, and the wine didn't hurt it at all.

Altogether, it was a memorable meal.

Then we went to our hotel, ¼ block away, and went to bed. It was Saturday night, and the night was just beginning for several thousand Spaniards who lived in the neighborhood. There was yelling and banging and singing most of the night, but it didn't bother me much. I like to know how other people live.

September 4

On Sunday morning (in Barcelona) we got the slip from the desk clerk, to entitle us to breakfast across the street (the street is more an alley). We went upstairs for breakfast.

We walked to the stamp and coin dealers' market in the Plaza Real, the square where we had lunch the day before. We meandered in the direction of the Royal Palace. After a little while we decided to go the rest of the way by Metro.

We went 2 stops, about a mile, and got out at the foot of the Royal Palace, which housed a great museum, to which we were headed. The Palace was about ¼ mile away, on a hill, and there were wide stairs all of the way up. The buildings on both sides were built for some 1908 (+ or -)

World's Fair, and currently being used for exhibitions.

We went into the Palace (by the front door). There were 10 or 15 people around, going to see the museum, and the rooms are so large, and there are so many of them, that you feel you have the place to yourself. It is free — They hand you a ticket. The pictures and jewelry in the Gothic half, which we went through carefully, but steadily, were very fun. The guide book said they were the best collection of Gothic paintings (in my mind one of the museums in Florence might have more), but there was room after room of very early Madonnas and Saints. One of the Spanish kings, perhaps Philip II, felt it was his job to preserve the treasures from centuries in which the Reformation was occurring, and he was in a very good position to do it, being the Holy Roman Emperor. There are many beautiful altar paintings from Germany, England, and Holland.

After two hours in that museum we wandered outside looking for the Archeological Museum.

We sat for a few minutes in the Royal Garden. We asked directions to the Archeological Museum, and they said to keep going, that we couldn't miss it. So after ¼ miles of downhill walking we came to it, from the back.

There is a very nice exhibit, lots of caveman utensils, and a careful explanation of the burial customs of the Carthaginians, and a non-trivial amount of Phoenician stuff: Astartes, stones with cuneiform, knives and other tools. We spent about ½ hour there, then walked back up the hill and had lunch (or dinner) in a restaurant whose sign we had seen on the way down.

After dinner we took the Metro to our hotel, The Catalunya.

Before we could catch the Metro, as we walked back from the Picasso Museum, we crossed in front of the Cathedral, which was beautiful in the twilight, and there were a lot of people walking around. We passed through and paused to look at the Picasso mural on the School of Architecture, when they put on the lights. The Baroque Cathedral lit up from below. Then the people danced the Sardana: They pile their luggage on the center of the circle, clasp hands, and make simple 2-step, raise and lower their hands on signals indiscernible to me. It is very gentle, and the circles were formed by people who were the same age. They all wore soft-shoes. The largest circle, in the center, was composed of important people, 26-32 or more, and they had a leader, who let people in the circle, etc. There were 10+ musicians in the band, and after 2 or 3 acts, a lady asked us for a contribution for the music. Some of the dancers were very old, 75+, and there were teenagers, upper-crust types.

Cathedral at Barcelona

Then we rested, for an hour or two, and went to an Italian restaurant. On the way home we looked at the lighted cathedral again. There are two angels, equally spaced about ½ the way across, that are very effective in the light show. They seem to hover over the whole proceeding, as if suspended against the sky, if you are standing in the right place. In the square the people danced the Sardana – piling their luggage in the center of the circle, making a simple 2-step, raising and lowering their hands via imperceptible signals, all wearing soft shoes. Beautiful.

Then home, and to bed.

Abbey at Montserrat, Catelonia

September 5

On Monday we went on a local tour of Montserrat.

When we got back we walked to our hotel, and after the usual agony over alternatives, went into a restaurant two or three doors down the street from the hotel. We ate among the busy Barcelona types, perhaps the only tourists. Then we finished dinner and went to our room and siesta'd a little.

Our plan was to go back to the Picasso Museum, which the guide book said would be open Monday afternoon. After a much more efficient approach, we arrived at the front door to learn — CLOSED MONDAYS. Crisis! — We decided to visit the Barcelona City Museum, which wasn't very far away, 200 yards +, across impossible city streets, down labyrinthine alleys, etc. But it was a lucky choice. We started with a 20 + minute explanation of the archeological excavation, in process, of the Roman city that is under the Cathedral. Only the old Roman wall had been there, and houses, and streets lined with drains. Then the Romans used it for a cemetery, so there are some grave stones, large buried urns, etc.

We went upstairs, and there are two or three floors of exhibits designed to convince you that Barcelona belongs in the proud group of Mediterranean super-cities: Venice, Florence, Marseilles...Their argument has merit. They were among the vanguard of the cities with elected representative city councils. The record books of the various guilds from the 14th, 15th, etc. centuries are there, with, for example, cloth designs registered by the weavers, building techniques registered by the ship-builders, etc.

There are original documents from the time of the siege by Napoleon's army, paintings, etc (1805+).

We went down after it was about to close, and ate at the all-vegetable restaurant across the street from the hotel, then took a walk along the Ramblas, along with several thousand other people. This is a 6+ block-long park in the middle of the main thoroughfare, which goes from the Gothic area down to the ship yards, where the Columbus statue is. As in the other

Columbus Monument, Barcelona

Mediterranean cities we have been in, the "corso" (evening walk) is a big part of everyone's life. There are flower stalls, tables for sitting and having a drink, etc., along the way, but everyone in town seemed to be strolling there. After about ½ hour we abandoned our seats.

As we wound our way from the City Museum to our hotel, we stopped and listened to a street musician, who played a concert by Quantz, accompanied by his hi-fi, which he had set up on one of the back corners of the Cathedral. We got there at about the beginning of the 2nd movement and heard him through. He was very good, and I think this is a superior way to practice. There is a live audience, and things are going on all over the place. The boy came in well on the harmonies, his breathing was good, and he had nice tone. We listened until the end, and then wandered along.

September 6

Some time Monday I had gone to a travel agency and bought a ticket on the through-train to Grenada (only one a day), to leave at 4:15 +/-, on Tuesday. We chose a 1st Class ticket, with reserved seats, but no beds. (This turned out to be a good choice, since no one else came to our compartment.)

I wanted to go back to the Picasso Museum in the morning, but we arrived there ¾ hour before it opened (error in the guide book), and so we decided to walk to see the Columbus statue again, so we could photograph the Pinsons for our son-in-law Mike. It was 9 o'clock+ and the city was waking up, slowly. Kids were going to school, people opening shops…a beautiful day, and after Mary Ann took her pictures, we walked along the public dock where Columbus' ship is, and looked at the boats tied up. There was a 40 ft+ sailing yacht from Los Angeles. We were unimpressed. So we got back to the Picasso Museum, and went through it again. My main reason for coming back was to buy some prints, which I did.

Picasso Museum, Barcelona

I liked the Picasso Museum as much the second time through. I hadn't missed anything, except a small room with the Picasso chronology. In some ways the museum is unimposing, but the visitors are a nice bunch: all of them having a good time, everyone learning things they didn't know. If a person knows he doesn't like modern art, he simply doesn't go to the Picasso Museum.

We figured we had time for the Maritime Museum, so we put our bags in storage at our hotel, checked out, caught the Metro for 2 stops, and went there, across the street from the Columbus statue.

The building is very old, having been a dry dock in the 1400's, but now the water level is down 10 feet or so. When we came in there was a special exhibit, the evolution of steam ships, with photographs and models of the top of the line Spanish ships (yachts of the kings) from 1850-1950. There were sample state rooms (the Queens'), photographs, and large displays (in Spanish, so only marginally helpful to me).

After we worked our way out of that we saw the major downstairs exhibit, a reconstruction of the galley from which Don Juan led the Spanish in the Battle of Lepanto. It has 30 oars on each side. There are 6 big display boards that describe the battle completely — One of the greatest naval battles there ever was. There men were on each oar. I couldn't lift the sample oar that was there. Horrible.

Then we went upstairs where they had the Columbus stuff: models of the *Nina*, the *Pinta*, and the *Santa Maria*, commemorative medals, old maps and charts. The exhibit had items from other voyages. Then Mary Ann got a picture of the painting of Captain Pinson. We bought some postcards, and off to lunch, sorely needed by now (1:30 +/-).

We ate lunch at a restaurant we had spotted on the Ramblas. Then back to the hotel, and we picked up our bags, and wrestled them to the train station, 2 hours early. So we had a long wait, on not very comfortable marble benches. I bought my first Spanish Coke for $1, but it was surprisingly cold. After a while we boarded the train, found our seats in 1st Class, and settled in for our 18 hour ride to Granada.

September 7

In the morning, the countryside was very dry. There is irrigation everywhere, but most places look as if it has been several years since it rained. Then about 10 o'clock we wended our way into the fertile plain which lies below Granada.

About 11 o'clock +/- we arrived in Granada, and worked our way under track 1, through the station to catch a taxi. We didn't have a hotel reservation, and that always provides some anxiety in a strange town when you don't speak the language. I finally found the little shop, about 100 feet from where I had parked Mary Ann, and the girl told me to try the Hotel Tilos, show up, they will have a room, etc., or phone anywhere, whoever answers the phone will speak English (nonsense). When I finally figured out where Tilos was, it was about 50 feet across the Plaza from the bench Mary Ann was sitting on. So I went in there, engaged a room, took up the luggage, and got advice for lunch. The lady who ran the desk was very nice, and helpful several times during our stay, as were her husband and daughter. (Of all the people I dealt with in Spain I liked them the best. She spoke a little English, and really tried to understand basic communication.) At any rate, she made an X on our map for the Nueva, to which we repaired at our usual unencumbered rate. We worked our way to the restaurant, and had a very good lunch at a reasonable price. We walked the 2&½ blocks back to the Tilos, and got instructions for riding the bus to the Alhambra. Somehow we found the bus stop right away, and rode the twisted path through narrow streets up the hill, and got off just above the Washington Irving Hotel. Then there was a ½ mile uphill climb to the upper entrance.

Our trip through the Alhambra was a little bit of a disappointment to me. I have read too much about it: Washington Irving and a long book from the Athens Library. It was every bit as beautiful as it is described — But we were never out of sight of at least 2 tours, we had been up all night, and Mary Ann was beginning to feel the effects of all of the walking.

We started from the top, with spectacular views of the city and mountains behind, and walked through the gardens and dilapidated battlements. There is open irrigation everywhere. We saw the palace, which is indeed a monstrosity, and threaded our way through more and more ruins. I began to think there was nothing else.

Alhambra, Grenada

But then we got to the Moorish Palace, and the famous fountains and pools. They are one of the wonders of the world, but it was never easy to look even at one thing, because of the swarm of humanity. You end up spending your time conjecturing the nationality of the person who has gotten between you and what you were looking at.

Finally, in the lower courtyard I flaked out. There was a semi-comfortable bench, and I suppose I fell asleep for a few minutes. At any rate I was able to bring my mind to repose, and put the fragments of unbelievable beauty together, and eliminate the multi-lingual jostling (worse than a football game), from my mental image. (I suppose I shall never be able to think of the Alhambra without the mob.)

As it became dark we retraced our steps to the bus stop, saw our bus going up, and waited interminably for it to come down. We went to the Tilos, and rested a little, sitting for a while at a table out front in the plaza.

We went for dinner to a restaurant nearby. Then home, to bed.

September 8

We had decided to go to the coast to go swimming if we could. We left our large suitcase with the lady at the Tilos, and with her kind instructions went to the bus station, to get the bus to Salobreña, which is perhaps the nearest town to Granada which is strictly on the beach.

Our bus trip was a twisty mountainous descent, complete with switchbacks, one-lane tunnels, a lot of traffic, etc. After 2+/- hours we arrived at the bus stop in Salobreña, with its sun shade and 3 or 4 slots for buses. Crisis! We still didn't have any idea about where we were going. So we walked 2 or 3 blocks looking for something, unsuccessfully, until we decided that the best strategy was to get a taxi. The taxi stand turned out to be right there, and the dispatcher served in the role of travel consultant, and we decided to try the Hotel Salobreña, on the road to Málaga. Our taxi driver whizzed us there, waited until we registered, and it was a very nice luxury hotel with a large pool right by the reception desk. Our room had a balcony, but we had to strain to see the Mediterranean, since there was a large tree right by the window.

We quickly got in our bathing suits and went down to see if we could get to the beach. But the beach was 1 km. away, down a dirt road, and we chose the pool, and swam there for ½ hour or so. On the edge of the terrace there was a fine view of the beach. It was about 4 o'clock, and I really wanted to swim in the sea, so I took off for the beach. I enjoyed my walk a lot, in the hot Spanish sun. Beside the road there were the usual remnants of continuous habitation that one sees along the coast.

The beach, when I finally got there, was rocky, pebbly, and finally, at the very edge, coarse sand. A man and his wife were fishing, but didn't seem to be catching anything. I went swimming, a hundred yards or so around a big rock. It would have been nice snorkeling, lots of rocks of different colors. The water was exactly right, there were colder patches. I would love to have tried a long swim, but it was a long walk back up the hill (Also I will never forget the sharks at Gibraltar — I didn't see any in the Mediterranean this time, but it's not that far away.). I don't remember nicer swimming. Then I walked up the hill, taking goat tracks to save a ¼ mile switchback.

When I rejoined Mary Ann at the swimming pool, it was about 5:30 or later. I got a beer, Mary Ann a gin and tonic (with lots of gin). We watched the twilight come down over the town of Salobreña, which is plastered on the back side of a massif, with an old fort on top.

A little after 8 we went in to dinner, and we had consommé, artichokes, fish platter, and ice cream (in a Dixie cup). Then we went back to the terrace and watched the stars come out, and the light on the sea, and the reflection of the lights of the hotel on the swimming pool. Then to bed.

Fuentes de los gigantes, Grenada

September 9

The next morning we went to breakfast early, about 8:30, and then went swimming, and about 11 checked out, to make our way back to Granada. There were no buses from Salobreña, but they left from Motril every half hour, and we got from the hotel to Motril by taxi. Our driver got us there exactly on time, and we hopped on the bus after running through the Motril bus station. The bus ride back to Granada was a repetition (only up instead of down). We came onto a herd of goats, and pushed our way through. But that only happened once, in a little town. There was a lot of traffic, and I was backseat driving (silently) but I was glad I wasn't driving.

We got back to the bus station, took the city bus back to the Cathedral area, our hotel, and out to lunch. We asked our reception lady for another recommendation for a restaurant, wandered around a little, and found it. We decided to go to the Flamenco that night.

We skipped supper.

Then we got a ticket to go to the Flamenco, the early show at 11:00. We were to report at the desk at 10:15, get on the bus nearby at 10:30, arrive at the place (bar) where the show was to be at 10:50. Then the bus toiled up the hill to a bar under the walls of the Alhambra, next to the Washington Irving Hotel. We filed into the room, which already contained 75+/- people, and were jammed into a bank of seats that had been left open for those on the bus. The crowd was composed of one busload of very old people (65+), one bus of families with children, about 6 or 8 of them between 4 and 10, and one bus which was assorted, with young people on dates, visiting English ladies, etc.

The performers came out: 2 male singers and the guitar guy, three seated girls, two younger and attractive, one slightly older and plump, and then standing, a very slender woman, 40+/-. The show started, and the youngest girl started, immediately at a crescendo. The performers were ranked by ability, the least accomplished first. The singers tell a little story, and then the girl dances, and the guitar plays all of the time.

Another man appeared for the final two sets. He was probably the best dancer — His set was very nearly modern dance — The story involved a wastrel who spent all of his money on lottery tickets.

Then in the finale the older man and woman did a Flamenco about a love triangle, the third corner being the singer. It became very explosive, but needless to say the thin gypsy man won out. Everyone had a good time, enjoyed the glass of sangria, and piled out after an hour or so, to go to our hotel.

We were the second off the bus, slipped home quickly, and to bed. We left Spain the next morning.

IRELAND

The pre-Christian western drift of civilization came to rest in Ireland. They had a respect for law, tribal identity, and cultural tradition. There is some truth in the phrase, "The Irish Saved Civilization," and it's a part of their racial memory.

The secret to survival, as a species and a country, is having a sense of humor, something the Irish have steadily maintained. Retaining one's traditions in the face of oppression is another key to survival.

Both of these are on display when one looks at the most popular form of Irish dancing, Step Dancing. In Step Dancing, the top part of the body remains immobile, while the bottom part dances away. This became the national dance out of necessity. When the English overlords would peer into Irish windows, all they could see were the motionless tops of Irish bodies. Underneath the windowsill, there was joviality, there was pleasure. There was dance. It's a funny-looking dance. So, both keys to cultural survival are on full, vivid display in the national dance of Ireland, Step Dancing.

Introduction To 1989 Trip To Ireland

In 1989 we went to Ireland, motivated by genealogical urges both specific and general. Specifically I wanted to extend the efforts of my father, who had located the grave of his great aunt, Honorah Breheny, in Ballymote, and search for traces of her father Philip. Generally, I was curious about the land from which my father's grandfather had emigrated. Mary Ann made our preliminary arrangements through All Aboard Travel, who arranged our flight, car rental, and first Bed & Breakfast lodging. After that, we were on our own.

Shannon, Ireland

September 3

The airplane took off quickly, through a layer of clouds. We were on the wrong side to see the Atlanta skyline, but the trees and lakes and streets of Dekalb County are always fascinating.

When we came into Shannon, we slid through the total cloud cover, and the green fields, and River Shannon popped out at us. We were quick off the plane, smoothly through the baggage pick-up and passport check, and first in line for the rental car. The lady gave us an Escort (instead of a Fiesta), which was very nice. We walked out to the parking lot and met our little car, a deep burgundy 4-seater, much like our Fiat 132 in size and power.

So I started out driving on the wrong side of the road for the first time. I was a little nervous, and Mary Ann was even more nervous, but at this point (after 3 days of it) it doesn't seem so bad (knock on wood).

The problem with driving here is that roads are very narrow, and used simultaneously for walking, bicycling, getting the herd to the pasture, or for grazing, or parking, and finally for automobiles. Frequently you must stop completely, to allow some traffic situation to resolve itself. The solution I discovered is to think as if I were on a bicycle, being prepared for the eventualities of that form of transport.

About a mile from the airport I managed to stall the car in traffic, when I missed the clutch of my small car. Then I couldn't get it started again, while cars were streaming around. Fortunately, Mary Ann noticed that the choke was pulled out, and when I pushed it in, we were on our way again. But solving problems in thick traffic is a rich experience.

Dunguaire Castle, County Galway

We buzzed off along the road to Galway, the trip taking 2.5 hours or so, past green fields, and minor industrial enterprises and many signs of the new tourism. There were signs for castles, and a golf course or two. Galway was very crowded because it was the first day of the races.

Sky Road, Clifden

Then, off to Clifden, along the edge of a national park, through a sparsely-populated area. After an hour or so we arrived there, about 3 o'clock, and the town was humming, I threaded my way through traffic, not without close shaves and stops to examine sign posts, and we located Sky Road, where our bed & breakfast was situated. Fortunately, Mr. Mullins had posted two very helpful signs directing us to Ardmore House. The drive was along a road which eventually became single lane. There is enough traffic so that this is interesting. When two cars, or trucks or buses met on Sky Road, one of them must back to one of the slightly wider spots and pull off. Even then, there may be only 3 or 4 inches separating the vehicles. We only met 3 or 4 cars this time.

We went back to our room at the bed & breakfast, and I slept for 30 minutes or so, before taking a walk on the beach. The Mullins' dog, a very nice sheep dog with hair in his eyes had a great time rowdying in the water and then shaking it off on us, was our accompaniment. It was a spectacular evening, and we could see the waves breaking on the other side of the bay, and the cliffs and islands and rocky promontories were shining in the setting sun. The beach is very rocky, with only small bits of sand, here and there, among the cobbles.

The cows were nearby, and their "traces" were everywhere.

Then we collected ourselves, and drove back to Clifden, to get our dinner. Both the book and Mrs. Mullins said that O'Grady's was the place we should eat, so we parked and walked around until we found it, asking directions in a store, finally. We had dinner there.

Then we drove home and went to bed.

September 4

On Tuesday morning we got up and had our first breakfast at the B & B. They have been all the same: orange juice, cereal, bacon and sausage, eggs, toast and jam, and coffee. This morning we also had porridge. Then we went on a tour of the coast road. It was an overcast day, and we started out with mist, but it cleared up. The drive along Sky Road was beautiful in the bright morning, with green islands and the mountains and cliffs on the opposite side.

We made our way through the town out onto the road along the coast. There was a lot of traffic, and at one place I came to a complete stop, with my left tires into the bushes to let a bus pass. There was less than an inch to spare, and the driver didn't like it, but he didn't hit me.

We soon came to the turn off for the monument for the spot at which Alcock and Brown crashed following the first Atlantic flight crossing, from Newfoundland to Ireland. They landed in a bog, not more than a mile from the coast. The monument is on a hill about ¼ mile from the exact landing spot. You can see the inlets in both directions, and it was a beautiful, gusty place. They made their flight in 1919, and it was an accomplishment the equal of Lindbergh's, though not so well publicized.

Then we went back along the road and in and out of towns, along the beach in a spot or two, and in the town of Gowla we came upon a crowd of people standing in the road. We inched our way through and discovered it was a funeral. There were about 50 people there, and 3 or 4 cars, and a hearse, and as we came through, the priest drove up in a car.

After 3 or 4 miles we came to a fork in the road, and the signs were in Gaelic, and the left road was not so good as the one we were on, and the right road was some better, so we assumed that the main road would be the better one. But after a mile or so, the road became a single track, very much in the back country, never very far from the ocean, with rocky bog-lands, and an occasional cottage. After a little less than an hour we completed the circle, and arrived at a crossroads we had been through earlier.

After dinner that night we went to the sitting room and had a long conversation with two couples, one a man from Sussex and his colleague, and a male professor at the University of Washington in Seattle and his wife. The Englishman met his colleague just after WWII, when she was a displaced refugee in Italy. They have kept in touch over the years. Apparently he has a wife and a son not related to his colleague, but we didn't pursue the matter.

The professor from UW is a bio-statistician, but he started as a mathematics professor. We talked vigorously for 1&1/2 hours, as the Englishman and his colleague left to go to Clifden to hear the music. You could read their English minds, "The Yanks haven't changed in 40 years."

At any rate, this was my first shot at being a seasoned traveler, swapping tips and stories with my fellow journeymen.

Ballymote

September 5

On Wednesday when we woke up it was raining, a fine misty rain, and following our farm breakfast, off we went to Sligo, and eventually to Ballymote. On the way we stopped in Westport, having our usual difficulty finding parking, but ending up very fortuitously by the public toilets, which seem to be about as good as public facilities can be kept. There is almost no graffiti in Ireland, and I don't remember this being the case in any of the other countries we have traveled in. Then we went to the tourist bureau and didn't transact any business, but were advised to book our rooms from Sligo. Then we ambled down the street, popped into a bank and changed some money, went back out and hopped into our car.

We drove for 1&1/2 hours, and there were some beautiful spots, and some crisis turns, and road construction and traffic as we approached Sligo. We were tantalized by being within 4 miles of Ballymote, but we didn't feel confident about booking a room there by ourselves. So we went into Sligo with the usual crises of city traffic, no parking places, etc., and found the tourist information. We parked in the lot by the cathedral, and walked next door to the tourist information, and the young lady booked us into a bed & breakfast at Ballymote, at Mrs. Hogge's. The drive to Sligo from Ballymote is about 10 miles, and there are two tricky turns, one of which we missed, and some construction with one way traffic through an underpass, with sign-wielders at both ends. When we got to Ballymote we drove past our place, and drove through town, and finally asked for directions at the gas station. We were about 100 yards away, and an hour early. We went back to the church and looked through the old Franciscan cemetery. It was wet, and impossible to read many of the stones. The cemetery and a ruined church right there date from the 1400s. Some of the stones were n the 1840s-1850s' though, and it was with considerable frustration that I looked for the grave my father had seen in 1964, trying to find the engraving on truly old stones. The Franciscan church had been destroyed by the Cromwell soldiers in the 1600's.

After an hour we went back, and were met by Miss Jennifer Hogge, who looked to be about 18, a pretty girl with lots of ringlets put in by the hairdresser. She showed us our room, and we went out to supper. On the way there we passed the priest, Father Flynn, and I ran back and asked if he would permit me to look in the church register for my ancestors. After a lecture, that church registers were incomplete, etc., etc., he told me that I could return at 10:30 in the morning and the sexton would allow me to search the register. He told me also that the Brehenys lived mostly around Keagh (Kesh), and that I should go there to the church to search.

Later, after dinner we went back to Mrs. Hogge's and we had a long conversation with her, and her husband. She is an attractive lady, about 45 I would say, a computer programmer at the electric company in Sligo, and her husband works in Sligo too. His father lived next door until he died, just recently. They gave us several suggestions of people we might talk to. There is a Breheny who works at the Post Office, and an old man at Kesh named Breheny. But we talked about raising children and simple, small-talk things like that. She told us she had another guest coming in the morning, who comes every year and stays a week. She was born in Ballymote, and married a doctor and lives on Long Island, but he is an invalid and the lady comes to Ballymote for a rest. We met her just before we left, and she told us she had gone to her school and found the records when she began the fourth grade.

September 6

On Thursday morning we had breakfast at 8:00, talked briefly with Mrs. Hogge, who was on her way to work, and started out to mail postcards. In the post office, we bought some stamps, and asked the postal official selling stamps if he knew any Brehenys. He said there are Brehenys all over Ballymote, and in the pub across the street one of the proprietors was the daughter of John Breheny. The pub is called Coleman's. There was a shop down the street run by Owen Breheny. So, I wrote my postcards, and it was almost time to look at the church records.

We went to the church, and there were about 30 people attending the service. When they came out, we saw the sexton by the sacristy, talking with the men who were repairing the roof. So we introduced ourselves, and he took us into a small room with a table and some chairs, and he brought the parish register of births, beginning in 1856 – going, I suppose, until 1870. So we read through all of the names and on page 6 found John Breheny, born 1857, whose father was James, from the village of Einlagmakton, which is about 4 miles from Ballymote. So when we found this, the sexton went back and got the family register from Einlagmakton, and looked up the Brehenys in there. There were two families of Brehenys, but no Philips.

The recording of the church register was very interesting, even exciting. There were some illegitimate babies, about 1 or 2 a page. An early entry listed the father only as the Duke's gardener, poor child. There were 5 Brehenys and numerous Kieltys in the register.

The register of births was a large book, say 20 inches X 15 inches, and a child's name, the name of his/her parents, and later in the register the name of the god-parents, the date of birth. The family register was a smaller book, with confirmation, whether the person died, or left the parish after the entry, etc. But these were entered by family, and there were two Breheny families in Einlagmakton. I was excited as I looked through the registers, and found the several Brehenys.

Then we drove up the hill to the newer cemetery. It was drizzling, but after about 20 minutes, and getting ourselves wet, we found the burial plot of Honorah Breheny that Dad had found when he was in Ballymote 25 years ago. She died when she was 80 years old in 1911, so she was born in 1831. Her son was Owen, and there is a son or grandson of his named Owen, who has a shop on Main Street.

Cemetery near Ballymote

Then we went to Coleman's pub, and I introduced myself as Tom Breheny. The proprietor is a young man, 30 years old or so, and he was very surprised. We talked about the possibility that Philip was from the town of Ballymote, but he thought we should go around Kesh. Then he introduced me to an elderly man sitting there, Andy Breheny. He may have been 70 or older, and he was sitting there having a pint of stout. I asked if he knew of a Philip Breheny, and he thought for a while, and said he didn't but that we should go to Kesh and talk to the people there. He told me that a lady had talked to him about her ancestors, and he had shown her the old farms, and she had been very happy to learn all the things he told her. Mary Ann was with me, and we were a little uncomfortable in the pub, at 11:30 in the morning. And we wanted to go to Kesh.

We made our way into Sligo, slightly easier this time, except for the excavation of the water pipes in front of the Tourist place. So we parked in a lot nearer to town, and walked back, got our tickets and a room. We went to Kesh, but without success.

Then we walked back to the center of town, which was busy, and crossed a bridge and saw the sign for the Genealogical Society, which is in the same building as the museum.

I went into the Genealogical Society, and the receptionist invited us to sit down, that the consultant would be along. After 10 minutes +/- he appeared. His name is Shane Gahaugn and he had lovely red hair and a beard. So we talked for a while, and he explained the limitations of the genealogical services he could provide, etc., and the places he could look, etc.

Then we looked at the museum, which had a couple of rooms of antiquities, some things from the Abbey at Ballymote, etc. There was a nice hoard of 15 or 20 silver coins, which were discovered recently (60s I suppose) in one of abbeys near Sligo. They probably were from the treasury of the abbey, and were hidden at the time the Cromwellians sacked it. The Independence Room had a lot of Yeats stuff, a panel of 6 or 8 photographs from his funeral. In addition there was a wall with a lot of things which had belonged to Lady Constance Markievicz [sic], who was very important in the independence movement. They had the clothing that she wore in jail, and a very fine portrait painted by her husband, as well as displays of several of the biographies that have been about her.

There were numerous pictures by Yeats' brother.

We went back to the car, and drove back to Ballymote in the afternoon rush hour. I was apprehensive about the construction area where they had two men posted, directing the one-way traffic flow. What would we do at night when they went home? (In reality, they left it so 2-way traffic could take place, a fact I discovered that night.)

We went and heard the music of a traditional Irish group.

The players assembled, a guitar player, an Irish drum, an accordion, to begin with. By that time there were 30 or 40 people assembled in the two rooms, and one table of mostly women were singing along. The drummer added in an important way, in some sense setting the tone of each of the songs. Everybody there knew everybody else, except for 4 or 5 other Americans, who were aficionados, more or less. The songs were lovely, some of them instrumental, and one or two were ballads, but it was not easy to hear the words. So we listened to 5 or 6 songs — I was ready for another beer, but since I was going to have to drive back to Ballymote, I resisted the temptation. Then we got up, and our seats were immediately grabbed by 4 or 5 people. We drove back to Mrs. Hogge's and went to bed.

September 7

On Friday we got up and had our huge breakfast, met the other guest, said goodbye to Mrs. Hogge, who went off to her work, finished packing, and paid our bill to Jennifer, and took off, to take some photographs of the old abbey, etc., mailed a postcard, and then bade goodbye to Ballymote.

Our goal was to see the ring graves at Carrowmore. These are on the north side of Sligo. While we were looking we went to the beach at Strandhill, got out and looked very briefly, trying to get good shots of the beach. The other side the mountain has the Tomb of Queen Mab on its summit. During the search for the old graves we circled the mountain, more or less. The graves are well sign-posted until you are there, and we drove by without knowing we were there. So we drove 3 or 4 miles past, then turned around and came back. The graves are in the middle of several fields, and consist of stones, about ½ the size of an automobile, say 20 or so, in a circle, with much smaller circles in some of them, and other recognizable stone groupings. This is the oldest and largest Stone Age burial ground in Western Europe. Only one or two have been excavated using modern techniques. They found 18 young women's skulls, with male bones adjacent. When we walked from the road to the circles we got our shoes wet, and one needed to be vigilant not to step in cow manure. It was a beautiful morning, and we looked at 2 or 3 of the rings fairly carefully, without understanding very well what we were seeing.

Then we headed for the Glencar waterfall. It is at the head of a narrow valley, steep on both sides with a long narrow lake in between. The road is very close to the lake most of the way, and at the end we stopped to take photographs, and fortunately discovered the path up to Glencar right there. We climbed about ¼ mile, on paved path to the waterfall.

Then we decided to work our way south to Lough Gill, and see Innisfree. The roads cross lots were narrow, as usual, and eventually diminished into the extreme one-lane for two directions case. Fortunately, there wasn't any traffic at all, and after one or two missed corners we came to Parke's Castle. This is now in a fairly advanced stage of reconstruction. We paid a pound each to get in, but it started with a very nice video, which explained briefly the history of most of the places we had just been, The Abbey of Ballymote, the rings at Carrowmore, the mound of Queen Mab, nearby Innisfree, etc. The restoration is proceeding slowly, and they have true artisans working on it, making floors with two inch hard wood planks, fine joining everywhere, etc.

After leaving the castle we drove around through the new Sligo development area, very large elegant new houses, on 1/2 acre lots. We came into town adjacent to the hospital, and then managed to lose the way, trying to find the bed & breakfast we had reserved. I asked a lady, and she directed us to a street about ¾ of a mile away. I still managed to make a wrong turn or two, but finally we found it. It was about 4 o'clock.

Mary Ann walked down the hill and left the laundry at a place near the parking, while I took a nap (and wrote in the journal). The trip down was pretty quick, but the trip back was strenuous, so Mary Ann said.

We went to dinner and then a play. When the play was over we picked up the car in the car park, in a rather tough looking area with a family living in a trailer nearby. I would never go into a place like that at 11:00 at night in Atlanta.

September 8

On Saturday morning, just before we left we had a very long conversation with our proprietor, about 1½ hours. We talked about everything, and showed her our pictures, and looked at her pictures. She is a red-headed woman, with 5 children, and she likes to talk a lot. We argued in principle about most things.

After it all, she advised us to go to the tourist place to make a reservation in Athlone. It was fortunate that we did, since the girl tried 3 or 4 places, and then sent us away to do some shopping. We bought some things for Patrick and Danny and talked to the proprietor of the store, who was interested in our reason for coming to Ireland, and he asked if I were a judge, and I said no, but the Brehons weren't really judges as we think of them today, rather traveling men called in to settle quarrels, and I said I had done that.

We went back to the tourist bureau and we had a room for the night, just north of Athlone, at a little village named Glassan. We drove down the Boyle road, and passed on the other side of the hill where the caves at Kesh are. There is a beautiful lake down below, Lake Arrow, and we stopped at a lay-by to take some photographs, and get a last look at country known to my great-great grandfather. From the top of the hill, where we were, this side of the mountain was prettier than the other side, but it may be that the elevation was the reason, or maybe the sunshine made the difference. It had been mist and drizzle the day before, when we were in Kesh. While we were driving we played the tape of Irish songs we had bought Danny, and it was beautiful to hear "On the shores of America I can still hear my sainted mother's song" or whatever. It must have been a truly brave man to leave it all behind, because, at least for the few days we were there, there were 40 shades of green.

After about two hours of driving we came to Athlone. Our goal was Clonmacnois, on the upper Shannon River, near where it joins Lough Ree. This was an abbey which was a great center of learning in the period from 1200-1500. The display was not extensive, but it was trenchant. As you went in there were several well-preserved grave stones, one for a scholar, one for an artisan, and some others. The young lady who sold us our tickets very nicely explained the stones. We read the panels of explanation, and went out in the churchyard to see the high crosses and the ruins of the abbeys and churches. It was a breezy day, and the sight seeing was vaguely unpleasant. The high crosses were mostly new, 1850-now, at least the ones you could read. The ruins are interesting, heavily pillaged by the Cromwellians.

In the area where we were, we were never more than 20 miles from the ruins of an abbey or church that was completely destroyed by

Cromwell's army. **It is easier to understand how the Irish feel about the English.** Following this, the English started a plantation system, with the Irish Catholics as serfs.

~

But then we walked a couple of hundred yards to look in the ruins of the old castle. It was a mess, only a few big features tilted and askew. We walked through the moat, and climbed a steep path, where we had a beautiful view of the River Shannon, and a small jetty with half a dozen boats moored. We walked down the far side, since the slope was less, and made our way back through the two tour bus crowds, one French, on Irish, to our nice car.

Our goal was to make our way to our B & B, and to avoid the center of Athlone, if possible. The map showed an ambiguous symbol that could have been a by-pass, but if there was such a thing there wasn't a sign for it on the road. So we made our way to the center of town, made a sharp right at the Hotel Hoey, and followed the directions given to us by the girl at the Sligo tourist bureau, and drove to Mrs. Demsey's. Mr. Demsey was working in the yard, and the children and dog were rowdying around on the lawn. We went in, unloaded, and were served tea. Soon we were joined by a young German couple, from Ulm, and we had a long conversation with them, a travelers' conversation. We talked about everything, conditions in the countries we have been in, the Common Market, overpopulation, war and peace. He didn't want to go to Yugoslavia, but he loved Spain. This was their first visit to Ireland. He was very Teutonic, but then I tend to be very American.

~

September 9

On Sunday morning we got up about 7:30, ate our huge breakfast about 8:30. After breakfast we put our luggage in our car and aimed for

Navan. There wasn't much traffic, everyone was in church, and first we went through Goldsmith country, at least that's what our map said. It was gently rolling, with villages, lots of stone walls and buildings, and green fields and copses.

Newgrange Burial Mound

We took off for Newgrange. The Newgrange Burial Mound is 3 or 4 miles from Slane down back roads, but well marked. There were two tour buses pulled up at the parking area when we arrived, and 10 or 15 cars. Walking briskly to the entrance, where we paid I pound to enter, we were given a yellow glue-on disk to indicate that we were to be in the 2nd group to enter the passage. We walked up the hill and heard the explanation of the tomb being given by a young college girl, presumably an archeology or anthropology student. The tomb is huge, the size of ¼ acre or more, and there are large stones around the base, 128 I think, cut rectangularly, in the proportion of bricks. Then there are a large number of stones, some grey and some white, piled in a semi-ellipsoid shape. The stone in front has three spirals carved on it. It is 3&1/2 feet high, and 10 feet wide. On the other side of the stone there is the entrance passage, through which the sun passes during the winter solstice, for 15 minutes a day, for 3 days, and lights up the central chamber. We were in the midst of a busload of German high school students, who were being (mild) pests. About 20 of us filed in to the central chamber and got a demonstration, using a flashlight, of what it looks like for 15 minutes in the morning of the winter solstice. The roof of the tomb was made of large stones, carefully interleaved so the tomb is waterproof. Each of the stones weighs 2 or 3 tons. There was a lot of decoration in the central chamber, and the two smaller side rooms. One of the stones had a replica of the spiral design on the stone at the entrance. When we filed out again, another group was getting the pre-entry explanation, by a different guide. Then we wandered around the outside of the tomb, looking at the stones that have been identified as having significance for the cremations that took place there. The man who carried out the reconstruction was named O'Kelly, and on the airplane home the man behind us told us he had been in school with him.

It was breezy and a little cold wandering around in the field. So we snaked our way outside the gate and into the tourist place, to use the facilities, and buy some postcards. Mary Ann had a long discussion with the girl at the reservation desk about accommodations in Dublin, but we weren't really near enough, I thought.

We got in our little car and took off for the Hill of Slane. That is a very holy place in Ireland, where St. Patrick first lit the Paschal fire, in 545 AD, to signal the Irish to assemble and be converted to Christianity.

Hill of Slane

We drove back to Slane, and up a side road for a couple of miles, finally along a single-lane to a parking lot, which was ¼ mile or so from the church and cemetery and ruins of the abbey. The grass was mowed by the cows, who left their traces, as was the case in most historical places we had seen. There were a lot of high crosses, of recent origin, and even some new graves. In the old church, which was a ruin, there were some old stones. The view across the Boyne really was spectacular, the river in the distance wound around the fertile valley. You can see why this is one of the first cultivated areas on the face of the Earth. We climbed over the abbey, and I went up some narrow stone stairs, but not as far as you could go. There were perhaps 10 other people on the hill while we were there, but no one was very close to us.

As we came down the hill there were two tiny children playing in the middle of the road, probably between 2 and 3 years old. There did not seem to be anyone around looking for them.

We went back to our B & B, and sat and talked to Mrs. Bagnall, the proprietress, for 20 minutes or so. She told us about her children, and there were about 20 or 30 awards for competition dancing on a table, and a big trophy or something, which had been presented to her husband when he was Lord Mayor of Slane. She advised us to have dinner at the castle, which was ½ mile down the road.

We followed her advice, and drove down the hill, and into the gate of the castles, where we parked our car. We went into the castle, and the first room was a large reception area with quite a few interesting prints and pictures on the wall, as well as the board from the bell system, for summoning the servants.

We went into a large dining room, 40 or 50 ft. long, with 8 or so tables set up, and a large bar. We were seated and I had beef stroganoff, spinach and blackberry pie, coffee, and beer. It was very good. Mary

Ann had pork filet with a cream and wine sauce, potatoes, and Irish Mist soufflé, a coffee. She thought this was her best meal.

We turned the wrong way going out and went through the coach yard of the castle, but ended up where we were supposed to be. So, back to our B & B and to bed.

September 10

The next day we drove through Dublin, past shopping areas, Georgian houses, parks, and playing fields, stadiums and churches, and finally arrived at the central bus station. We took our luggage about 20 feet to a taxi, and drove a mile or so to the B & B at 113 Anglesey, Mrs. Doran's. We were met at the door by a young man, who showed us our room and gave us very good instructions about how to catch the bus, which, after a reasonable interval, we did.

Donnybrooke Church, Dublin

The No. 10 bus, which we caught at the Donnybrooke Church, took us to the center of town. As we strolled along, we crossed Abbey

Street, and a sign to the theater which was right there. I went to the box office, and the young lady said there was a Yeats show tonight in the Peacock, which is a smaller theater in the same building as the Abbey Theater. So this was the last full audience "dress rehearsal" for the play, *The Cuchulain Cycle,* which was the most important feature of the symposium for the 50th Anniversary of the death of Yeats. So we got tickets for 7:30 that evening. The opening night for Tuesday in the Abbey Theater was sold out.

As we entered the National Gallery, someone said, "Mary Ann," and it was Ann Howe, whom we had seen changing money in Atlanta. They were on their day off with their tour, and we compared notes for a few minutes, their out-pointing us on the *Book of Kells*, which we had not seen, and Branch directing me to look at the "Proclamation of Independence," a copy of which was on display just beyond the Book, so I got some points back by asking, "Was that the one drawn up in the Post Office in 1916?" and they didn't know.

We spent an hour in the gallery, which I enjoyed, and there were many fine pictures, Gainsboroughs and Turners, Renaissance religious paintings, in some sense representations of everything, but no rooms full of the same guy, and adjacent pictures were frequently in clashing styles, etc. There was a substantial Picasso, from 1924, next to a Juan Gris, which isn't fair to Gris. There were two nice Monets with an insubstantial Picasso in between, etc. In the several rooms of Irish paintings there was a room with 20 or 30 works by Jack Yeats (Yeats' brother). His caricatures of Irish types were nice, but his work went through several styles, never confidently plowing a furrow, always a bit derivative.

We walked back to the front of Trinity, and caught a No. 10 bus, got off at Donnybrook, and walked the hundred yards to our B & B, where we snoozed a little, and changed for dinner and the theater.

As we dashed along through the 7 o'clock crowd, Mary Ann asked, "Do you **have to** run?" So I slowed up, and we reached the theater with a few minutes to spare.

We sat in the back row of the Peacock, a theater with seats for 150+, with say 85-100 people there. *The Cycle*, consisting of 5 one-act plays depicting incidents from the life of Cuchulain, a legendary Irish hero, is staged poetry, and was very strong. The dancing and music were excellent, and the performance made a complete change in my desire to know what's in Yeats. Somewhere in my Irish tour I read a paragraph or two by Yeats describing his view of the purpose of the motions of the actors during a drama, and he said that this too should be poetry. And so it was.

The difference between the company here, and the students in the play at Sligo was substantial. And the play was equally that much better.

Cuchulain was a great Irish warrior who liked the girls, and this was his downfall. I don't understand all of the presumed comparisons with the struggle for Irish independence, but some of it is obvious. Perhaps I will go back and read it.

At any rate, I was entranced by it all, and fell in love with Cuchulain's mistresses, even if they were witches.

Then we slipped out and found a No. 10 bus, which was lucky, because when we got to the Donnybrooke Church we learned it was the last bus of the day.

Then thc 100 yards to our B & B, and to bed.

September 11

On Tuesday morning we had our own breakfast, served by the daughter of the house, a girl in her next to last year of pre-college school. I asked her if she liked school, and she said "Yes," and I said, "Really?" She said, "That's where all my friends are." But she has 4 or 5 older brothers, and 3 or 4 are in the University, so I suppose that is why they have to run this B & B. They had a large number of elegant things in their house, and some Ladro figures. The silver was sterling, and I had the impression that her father was a doctor, without any evidence that this was the case.

We went down to see if they had re-opened the museum, and they had, so we were in good shape. They started our tour with a video which was a brief summary of the history of Ireland with photographs of some of the more important things in the museum, e.g. St. Patrick's bell, a missal which had belonged to St. Colomba, some gold neck pieces and brooches.

Then we walked around and saw a lot of things, and read all of the explanations. There was a room or two from the Viking invasion around 1000 A.D. The Viking village in Dublin was the site of a very thorough archeological study. *Most museums have one first-rate macabre item.* Here it was a skull of a man who had been killed with a sword, with 3 huge pieces of his skull sliced off. But there were hundreds of artifacts, utensils, and items from daily living, as well as armor and weapons.

We finished the museum in the Independence Room. This contains the artifacts from the 1916 uprising. The presentation is not very understanding relative to the British point of view. They were in the middle of the greatest war there had been, and the Irish were being armed by the Germans. The British were ordering the cream of their population to walk into the machine guns of the entrenched Germans. They had been gassed, and the upper reaches of the British command were strictly hysterical.

No thousand year quarrel has a simple resolution.

But the Irish Rebellion of 1916, while the necessary symbolic gesture, was not the heroic display of inevitable social upheaval that the display would have one believe. *Undistilled hatred is not an end in and of itself.*

Ahh, the Irish are specialists at the sad song. (Sad songs make me cry.) And this display was about as sad as you can get. The insurrectionists were executed, more or less summarily. All the letters which permitted the mothers of the leaders to visit them the day before they were executed are on display, etc. Pictures of them being marched away after their captures, etc. One beautiful photograph of the bunch in the main Post Office firing on the besieging British Army. And, as always, there were some nice photographs and artifacts of the Lady Constance Markievic [sic].

Irish independence, as with all independences, did not occur without considerable bloodshed. Still, I think it has finally happened. The residents of Northern Ireland have their rights, and the modern world can envisage a Protestant minority in a land the size of Ireland.

When we left the museum, at my request, we searched for a coffee shop and had tea and rolls, as a lunch substitute I suppose. There was a shop about 50 ft. up a side street, and we could have a deli lunch, but didn't.

Then I went to the Genealogy Office, adjacent to the museum, while Mary Ann went shopping. In some sense this was the high point of my tour, so I hope there are enough pages left to describe my genealogical experience.

I went into the office and sat down and talked to the receptionist, who explained the role of the genealogy consultant, and the cost (10 pounds). So, after a little thought I paid her the fee and she called the consultant who was in rotation, Sean Murphy, a young man with red hair and a neat red beard. He took me to a table in the room, and told me that 10 pounds entitled me ½ hour of his services. He was very businesslike, and didn't want to waste very much of our time listening to my side of it. He prepared a page with my instructions, writing as he explained.

The four steps that he outlined for me:

1) Search the Townlands Index, 1851
2) NLI Index of surnames, County Sligo
3) Griffiths Valuation for the parishes indicated by steps (1) and (2)
4) Search parish registers in the Ballymote area for births, marriages, etc.

All of this could be started in the National Archives, located not more than 2 miles away. Mary Ann came in as I was finishing my consultation. He probably gave me some extra time.

So we said goodbye, and walked out, not sure of what we should do next. We decided that I should go to the National Archives, and that Mary Ann should shop, and meet me there in 2 hours.

I walked briskly toward the National Archives, crossing the Liffey on the footbridge, and didn't need directions until I was nearly there. I asked one man outside a pub where the National Archives was, and he didn't know, even though they were less than ¼ mile away. (I have observed this phenomenon before.) So I entered a building, which was a court, and got directions to a gate 50 feet away. I went in the gate, found the Archives by myself (a first), applied for my permit, and signed a statement that I had read the rules, and the helpful young man at the desk read my sheet, and called for the volumes I needed. So I went and sat down, and in 3 minutes the book appeared.

Then I started looking at the indices and the other book. There were Brehenys beginning on the first page. So I copied it all out onto the backs of pages that the genealogist had provided.

I tried to be careful to begin with, labeling the names I found with county, parish and community, both Brehenys and Kieltys (Kielties). But it seemed clear that I would not get through the books I had checked out, so I worked feverishly, copying 23 entries from *Griffith's Townlands Index of the Valuation, 1851*, which gives the number of times the name Breheny is mentioned, and Kielty in a given "townland."

Then I turned to the valuation itself, which contains first names. I copied these names down, together with the location of the land being taxed, and the 7th Breheny I found was Phillip Breheny, on page 49. He came from the Parish of Kilshalvy, the town of Killined, and on page 51, I found an entry for:

{Phillip Breheny, the town of Taunagh}

{Barthw., Breheny, land and house 18 acres—10 pounds, 10 shillings}

Since these towns are adjacent, I conjectured that there was only one Phillip.

The "Town of Killined" entry had no house, and was 6 acres, valued at 2 pounds, 10 shillings. In the town of Tawnagh there was a Michael Kielty listed.

I was so excited I could barely contain myself. A woman seated beside me asked to look at one of the books I had, which was OK by me. She acted like a professional genealogist. Mary Ann came along and I showed her the entry, and she copied some entries from the Parish of Englaghfed onto the page earlier in the journal.

So after I had been there 1½ hours or so, we left and walked across the bridge, and I examined St. Patrick's church in the distance, and we located Rudyards, that we had failed to find the day before. It was too early to eat, so we repaired to a pub, and I had a couple of pints of beer, and Mary Ann had a glass. Then we walked up the street to Rudyards, and I left my umbrella behind, but was able to go back and retrieve it.

After eating, we caught the No. 10 again, and returned.

September 12

On Wednesday, we started the day with another big breakfast, but had no goal but to get in the airplane on time. So we called a taxi, with the intent that he put us on the bus, but he suggested that he would take us to the airport for 10 pounds, and I said OK. He and I traded jokes on the way to the airport, something I have almost never done. He said I was happy to be going home. We drove by his house and pub.

We checked in at the airport. There was a security check, the man opened and pawed around in our suitcases. Then we went back and looked around the airport shops a little.

On the flight back we ate, saw the same movie they showed the other way, only listened to some of it this time, a Clint Eastwood ("Pink Cadillac"). We craned our necks to see some of the coast of Ireland, and various coastal scenes on this side.

Finally we landed in Atlanta, and Rusty was there to meet us, having come directly from work. We spent about an hour with Elizabeth and Rusty and the boys at Laurel Post Drive, and then drove home.

The End

FRANCE

Gaul is no longer divided into three parts. France has such a long and varied history that it is difficult to summarize. The traditional enemy of England, France and England fought so many wars and skirmishes against each other before the 20th century that it is difficult to accurately tally them, though they were allies in both World Wars. France is beautiful and ancient, thriving and modern, exquisite and difficult.

Introduction To Our 1990 Trip To France

THIS IS THE JOURNAL OF OUR TRIP TO FRANCE THIS FALL, THE FOURTH FALL TRIP TO EUROPE WE HAVE TAKEN IN THE PAST FIVE YEARS.

This year it has been very difficult to stay resolved to go; when the Iraqis invaded Kuwait, and in the month of hostage manipulation, the question is always there, is the proper place for a person at home, saving money and options in a possibly changing world? On the other hand, the world should not grind to a halt at the whim of an irrational dictator of a small country, drowning in overpopulation, which has run out of money.

I prepared for my trip by re-reading everything I could find at home about the WWII campaign in Normandy. This included pocket books about (1) D-Day, (2) the whole Normandy campaign, (3) the Encyclopedia Britannica, (4) the story by A.J. Liebling, etc. At any rate, we began today with the last 1/10 of the packing, and closing the house for 2 weeks. Then we sat around and talked (how to remodel the kitchen, Hemmingway, etc.) for about an hour, and then off to the airport. Danny drove, and will keep the Mazda for us.

We hopped out at the Delta, gave them our suitcases, changed dollars to francs, then proceeded to the T2 gate, to wait without incident. The airport seemed less crowded than usual. The plane loaded on time, but there was a delay while we waited for the 5 o'clock (airport) traffic. Our plane was smaller than the last 2 or 3 we have flown on, with 2 seats on the outside, and 3 across in the middle. It was new, and there have been some minor improvements – the reading lights were better, the signals for the restrooms work better, etc. We were adjacent to a bilingual family: a girl 6+/-, a boy 3, and their mother, who had a very American accent, but could shout in French. The 6-yr.-old was a smart girl who let me look through her kaleidoscope toy. She was very well-behaved, and wanted to know if I watched the movie in English or French. (I watched in English, she in French.). The pilot pointed out the lights of Philadelphia on the horizon to the right. I awoke when it was dawn and they were pushing breakfast (continental) on us. Later on we saw England and then the Channel, and the White Cliffs (Dover), and before we knew it we were landing at Orly Airport.

The airport is pretty well-organized – you must walk ½ mile to the luggage pick-up, but that gives them enough time to get the bags in. They stamped our passports, but it took less than 30 seconds. The two girls at customs looked the other way as we went through. The airport wasn't very crowded – the people were young – a lot of them teenagers – there was a black youngster with a big professional case for tennis racquets – and several bunches of Africans. We got to the baggage pick-up and our bags hadn't come, but there weren't any carts nearby, so I cruised almost the whole length of the airport before I found a waif cart, and hurried back with it, by which time Mary Ann had rescued our bags and was wondering if I had stopped for lunch (time to find cart 10-15 minutes). Then we went about 50 feet to the car-rental (Europacar), and the girl wasn't too organized. She had just gotten there, but she finally got us all punched in to the computer (300 key strokes, +/-, estimate), and pointed out the big window to the Europacar shuttle, and sitting behind this (waiting for us) was a sample of the type of car we had rented, so we could decide if it was OK. All of this was about 30 feet away outside of the window, but to walk to it was ¼ mi., since you had to go to the end of the airport to get outside, and come back. So I was glad I had the cart, even though the luggage is reasonable this time. It turns out that our car was brand new (only 12 km. on the odometer). I still do not like familiarizing myself with a new car in high-density traffic, but this is my

3rd time (my Fiat in Italy [1971], the Escort in Ireland [1989], and the Renault 105 this year), so I am beginning to get the hang of it. Our route was on the superhighway toward Paris until we got to the Paris perimeter (*peripherique*), then to the left on that for 20 miles or so, then off on the superhighway to Rouen. We were very fortunate in that the man behind us at the car rental was an American who totally knew, (1) how to do what we wanted to do, (2) how to tell us efficiently how to do it.

I hadn't yet mastered REVERSE in my Renault. At any rate, we tooled along the superhighway and in about 2&1/2 hours were at the turn-off to Pont Audemer (180 km. down the road in Normandy), the location of the B&B at which we had reservations. There were two or three nice things on the superhighway: two bridges, very close, first over the Eure, second over the Seine, very near their confluence.

We figured out not to go into Rouen, and (crisis) skipped the first (back road) turn-off to Pont Audemer, and got off with about 10 km. left to go, into secondary roads through flat fields, almost by ourselves. Driving on the right side of the road *is* easier.

Pont Audemer canal

Finally into Pont Audemer. We had elaborate instructions on how to get to our B&B, on a type-written brochure that the lady sent us at home, but no matter how good, instructions can be tough. Also, it took us time to discover that the French put an arrow just beyond a corner when they mean to follow that arrow at the <u>next</u> corner. So, after going the wrong way into a one-way street, pulling off and not being able to get the car in REVERSE (about 5 mins), when pulling and yanking, etc., it slipped in (I still don't know why) we got on the road to Lisieux, looking for the critical sawmill to turn by. (*Everything* looks like a sawmill when that is the key to your directions.). Finally we found a sawmill with big logs in the yard, and stacks of boards all around, and 150 m. beyond an almost hidden private drive, which led down a narrow bridge and up the side of a hill to our B&B. It was wooded, and green, past an abandoned barn. It is advertised as an 18th century gentleman's estate, and it is rather pleasant. We stayed in a detached building with 3 rooms, which is from the same period. The room was large light and two large windows looking out onto the estate, down the hill.

It was quarter to 11 when we got there. So we slept for about 2 hours, and decided to go for a walk in Pont Audemer. This is a very pretty little town, and is known as a market town, so there are lots and lots of little shops with everything you can get at the mall, but the people live near or above their shops, and there is a town square, with cafes and sidewalk bars around it, and an old church (11th century) and old alleys back in with nice houses. There is a small, swiftly flowing river (30 ft wide) which we walked along for 2 or 3 blocks, where we came to the tourist bureau. I asked the young lady if she knew how to get my car in REVERSE, but we never did make it. She was nice, but she truly did not know how. It was an interesting problem in communication, and she finally directed me to a garage (which was not what I wanted). We walked back through town, and bought two rolls to tide us over until dinner. We wended our way back to the train station, where we had parked, and following someone's suggestion (MA's or the girl at the tourist office) we got out the book about the car, and there it finally was—You must *lift* the 2nd little rubber gasket with 2 fingers to get the car in REVERSE! And I had accidentally done this, not once, but twice (under extreme pressure), without learning the secret.

So we drove back to our B&B, and slept for an hour or so, and then took a short walk about the premises. So it was an acre or two, with a very nice spring, with a 15-ft square holding pool which looked old, and some 200-yr. old trees, and lots and lots of new trees planted. We walked up some little paths until they became overcome with nettles. From the hill behind the house you could see across the valley, and to the edge of town, which wasn't that far (2 miles or so).

We had asked for directions to a restaurant, and our hostess gave us cards for two, and we chose one called Les Cloches, which was on the road to Rouen. So, we started out as the sun was sinking over the horizon, hunting for who knows what and where. Fortunately, the traffic had dwindled considerably, and we found the road to Rouen (the superhighway went there, too), but we tooled along the road, and at about the right distance was the town, and after going around the square there was Les Cloches...looking just like the sketch on the card. So I guessed the parking must be in back, and we drove in, and there was 1 space left. We went to the front, and the 8 or so tables on the glassed-in porch were occupied, but the young head waiter led us to a back room, which had 6 tables, not yet being used. It was a very nice Norman room, with a tile floor, prints on the wall (in the style of old books), and wild flowers on the table. So the place had 3 Stars in the book, and it was excellent. I had salmon pate', chicken in cream and wine sauce, with noodles and mushrooms, cheese (Pont d'Eveque) and pear cake with raspberry sauce, and a bottle of sparkling cider. Mary Ann had a small melon filled with brandy, salmon with caper sauce, some other cheese, and the same dessert. And coffee. It was very good, and it is a great experience to dine with haute cuisine. It took us an hour and a half. A young French couple sat at the table next to us, and she was pretty and he was handsome, and they were having a very good time, talking low. They had ½ bottle of wine, and a bottle of mineral water, so you can do it that way.

A bottle of cider doesn't have as much alcohol as a bottle of wine, I think, but at any rate, when I got to the car, I felt pretty normal. I maneuvered my car out of its narrow space, learned how to turn on the lights, and off through the dark. We went along pretty well until we missed a turn in the middle of Pont Audemer, and went along in the dark for 2 or 3 miles before we were convinced that this darkness was different from the darkness that should have been. So we retraced, and located the point of error, and this time the sawmill in the dark had logs in the yard, and we got to our B&B, about 10:30 pm.

September 5

We woke up in the morning later than we thought we would—MA at 8:00, myself at 8:20. Since breakfast was scheduled for 8:30, I shaved as fast as I could, and we made it by 8:37. We ate in the main house dining room (continental with fresh orange juice and home-made jam) and talked with Mme Denise Carel, who was old with a cane. The house had been in her family for a long time, was built during The Directory (between The French Revolution and Napoleon). The room was 16 ft. high, and had a full (or almost full) length window, and some old paintings, and some very old dishes on the wall. There was a stuffed crocodile on the wall in the hall, etc. It was interesting to imagine oneself eating there in the old days, especially as the largest painting was one of several musketeers being served a meal by a young maid, in such a room.

We packed up our bags, eased the Renault down the path, and got on the road back to Deauville about 10:30 AM, and there was quite a bit more traffic, vacationers and resort types. There was a film festival in progress (50 years of Bugs Bunny was a big entry), and a very nice sports car on display, the prize of a drawing.

We drove the coast road, sometimes 50 feet from the water, past the casinos, and campgrounds, and hotels and condos and real estate offices. Some 2-bedroom apartments, in pretty large 3-story buildings were +/-$70,000, etc. At some places there were hundreds of beach changing rooms, each 10-ft wide or so, along the edge of the beach. I suppose one rents them, has a picnic, spends the day...

The beach road from Deauville to Ouistreham is pretty well built up, a few empty places, and some of the time the road is on top, along the ridge, going through pastures, an occasional cornfield, etc. As we approached Ouistreham we came up to a 3-vehicle accident, which could not have been 10 minutes old, with a recreational vehicle in the middle, and a fairly big car having smashed into its rear end in good shape, a 3-ft. hole knocked its back end. It was hard to guess what had happened in broad daylight on a straight stretch, but probably it was a sudden stop crash.

At any rate, being a in a silly accident is a true worry. About ½ the cars tailgate, aggressively letting you know they want to pass, even a t 10 km. over the speed limit. It is not that much worse than Atlanta, except there are more of them. Also, when you are being given instructions on navigation, or requesting them, the tailgating is simultaneously in progress. So one occasionally misses a scenic wonder, such as a long view of the beach, or a family campground...

Near Ouistreham we stopped at a monument for Sword Beach, one of the British beaches. This was the western end of the Debarquement, and there are a large number of monuments and private museums in the next 50 miles. I suppose by now (Wed. night) we have examined closely 5 or 6 monuments, but have not yet gone into any museums, although we got to the door of one in a Quonset hut, and decided to pass it up, since we have scheduled the big museum in Bayeux for tomorrow. Our

Omaha Beach

goal was to check in to the Hotel des Marines in Port-en-Bessin, use the facilities, and proceed from there.

We worked our way in to Port-en-Bessin, inched our way along the quai, in an enclosed tidal pool in which the water level is maintained with a lock, around the corner from our hotel. The parking is on a pier, into the artificial harbor created by two large breakwaters.

So we parked, checked in, and off on a walk along the cliffs above Omaha Beach. We climbed up a pretty good cliff, to examine the remains of the German defense system. There were pill boxes, and cement gun emplacements as big as a 2-car garage, and miles of meandering trenches, which run along the top of the cliff here. It was high tide, and along here there was no beach for 2 or 3 miles.

The cliff was 100-200 ft., straight up, so there was no way soldiers could invade along there. There were gun emplacements all along. In the distance, you could see Arromanches, the remnants of the artificial harbor are still there in the water 45 years later, and it is impressive to see them 2 or 3 miles away. It was a beautiful slightly overcast, breezy afternoon along the cliff, with occasional bright sun. The ocean was very calm, hardly a ripple. There was an occasional small boat, like an outboard, but for practical purposes the ocean was empty. So we came back, looking in the cement fortifications, filled with litter and worse, and tried to figure how they were meant to be used. But then, after about an hour we came back to our car, and took off on the marked Tour de Plaza Dembarqument (or something). So, out through town, past the Omaha Beach Golf Course (!), through the little towns, to a place where there was a big monument to the US 1st Army. Near this monument was the emplacement of the enfilading big gun, which had 12 feet of concrete toward the sea, which the invaders did not know was there. These guns were responsible for a measurable fraction of the damage done on D-Day. They knocked out scores of tanks and landing craft. The soldiers coming in had to go through the 5 little fishing villages, since the cliffs were a total tank barrier everywhere else. The beach at low tide is 200 ft. or so more, and this had been covered with anti-tank hedgehogs, barbed wire, cement tank obstacles to which mines had been attached, etc. But there is very little visible of all this now. We walked down the beach. There was a campground right there, and 10 or 15 people on the beach, probably tourists, and 15 or 20 cars parked along the road above the monument. Everyone I saw there was French, although a little later we met a guy (my age) from Houston, who had his own guide. The guide wasn't very pleased when he talked to us. This was all at our next stop, at the monument for the National Guard. I walked to the end of the beach, and up the cliff at this end. This was on the end near Ponte de Hoch, but not quite there (a mile or so). The American cemetery is there, with 9500+/- graves. We drove through the parking lot of the cemetery, in which there were 200+/- parked cars, and 10+/- tour buses parked, but I have no idea where the people were, or what they were doing.

We continued on the tour, but before long decided it was too far to Ste. Marie d'Eglise (20 mi+/-), so we turned around and started back, hopping out at the Quonset hut museum mentioned earlier. I was beginning to need gas, so after 5+/- miles there was a modern looking station. I pulled up at a pump, and after 2 or 3 minutes a teenaged girl came out who pumped 107 F worth into my tank ($23+/-), which didn't fill it. So I have come 350+/- km. in my nice new rental Renault 5, at a cost of say $30 for gas. We drove back to the hotel, went to our room, and back to the streets of Port-en-Bessin, to buy 3 postcards, and look in the shops.

It is easy to believe that tanks could go along the roads into Port en D., which is what happened, at H+24 hrs., or around then. So we walked along the quai again, back to our room, and a short nap before supper.

I put on a tie for supper, and we went down one flight of stairs to the dining room. I was the only one with a tie on, which was different from the night before. The dinner cost ½ as much, and was about ½ as good. I had some very small oysters, some fish with boiled potatoes, carrots and zucchini, then camembert, then flan and coffee. MA had "mixed fruits of the sea" which were periwinkles, some very tiny shrimp-like critters, and some larger shellfish, the size of a small plum, that had to be extracted from the shell. As we ate, the breakwater filled up. It took about 1+½ hour to do it. When we sat down the tide was low, and two men were walking at the entrance, harvesting fruits of the sea of some sort and putting them in a bag. The water was just above their knees, more or less. As the tide came in the boats that had been resting on the bottom floated up. The change in colors from light blue to darker is beautiful to watch; this was the best thing about dinner at the Hotel de Marine – the big glass windows looking out into the harbor. After dinner we walked out along the quai, and watched a big boat preparing to go out, surely for several days. The young wives or girlfriends of the crew were standing by, a long wait I suppose, since they attached the electric cord to one outlet on the lamppost as we watched. The boat leaving was not next to the quai, but next to next to it, and everyone was hopping across the intervening boat. They had their nets wound up on huge reels, with power to reel them out and in, and big (bigger than a car door) roundish iron sleds to hold the nets down in the water. As we were leaving a somewhat smaller sea-going fisherman came in, and they turned the bridge over the tidal lock to let it in. The bridge rotates on a central post, very nicely, on instruction from a man in a nearby office, on the far side of the quai. Having survived all the excitement Port-en-Bessin could offer in one evening, we went to the hotel and went to bed.

September 6

We woke up in the morning at 7:45+/- am and I shaved and showered, and we went down to the bar for our continental breakfast, some toast and a croissant, and apricot jam (from a huge can I suppose) and *cafe au lait*. Mary Ann had chocolate (to try it). It is enough for breakfast, and not that much different from cereal. Our plan was to go to Bayeux to see the tapestry, and the WWII museum there.

We wandered around somewhat inefficiently following TAPISSERIE signs, when we would have been much better off following signs (if there had been some). But we got to see some back streets of Baycux which we might not have seen otherwise. After about ½ hour we came to a religious enclosure, and walked through to the building which houses the tapestry.

The Bayeux Tapestry is indeed one of the landmarks of western civilization, and there isn't enough space to say much about it here. This is the only record of the "Norman Invasion" of England in 1066, and the exhibit that precedes the viewing of the gigantic tapestry is informative, and there are full-page explanations of almost every panel in 700+/- ft. explanation that precedes the tapestry itself. In addition to the diagrams and textual explanation, there are several life-size figures: typical soldiers, William at his coronation, a typical worker lying around against a tree, etc. Also there are some small doll-size village scenes (a William the Conqueror doll house). We were there 3+/- hours, and I truly ingested much history that I hadn't known. (We bought some books and postcards, and I recommend them, and of course, the tapestry itself, to anyone who might be interested).

The Bayeux Tapestry is both an extraordinary work of art and a remarkable historical document. The abundance of imagery impresses the viewer. There are 626 characters, 202 horses, 41 ships, and 37 buildings. Since its creation, between 1070 and 1080, arrogant historians who have questioned the authenticity of its historical detail have, to a one, been proven wrong. Its depiction of military history, naval detail of the time, tools, and everyday life in the eleventh century is awe-inspiring. The Bayeux Tapestry's almost cartoonish style has kept the interest of tapestry viewers and curious travelers for nearly a millennium.

Bayeux Tapestry detail

Then we set out for the WWII museum, but Mary Ann said we had to see the cathedral, which was begun in the 11th century, but my initial shock of Gothic cathedrals has been overcome, and I can't think of any sensible comparison theory that I want to pursue. The stained glass is different from place to place, clearly, but how to put this in a single line of thought is beyond me. There aren't any rooms anywhere as high and ornate as those in cathedrals, but I don't think that line of thought led anywhere — I hope this is not the idea that led to the Super Domes of modern sports entertainment.

When we came out there was a very slight misty rain, which wasn't even clothes-dampening, rather pleasant actually, but such a rain can rapidly advance to a downpour, so (crisis) we walked quickly the 5 or 6 blocks to our car to get our raincoats. The pre-noon traffic was fierce, so after a lengthy conference we decided to walk to the WWII museum. I studied the city map provided by the lady at the Tourist Bureau, and we went straight there (not without questioning, of course, since in Europe it is not always easy to tell what is a street and what is not). We walked in the door precisely at closing time, 12:30 AM (contrary to the guide book, which said "open all day through September" — Crisis). What to do? So we retraced our steps, through Charles de Gaulle Park, and after some agony, decided to look for a tea shop. But Bayeux was truly closed down, only one or two persons in sight in the middle of the business district. The bakeries were open, and one teenage hangout with Cokes and egg sandwiches, which was vetoed because of flies, so we walked back to the car.

The museum was laid out with one side of the room full of newspaper clippings and photographs and small artifacts, and parallel, big displays of models in uniforms of the units involved, and larger items, weapons, vehicles, etc.

There were 4 or 5 rooms of this, again too much to describe. My understanding of this battle is by now pretty advanced, at least enough to spot the bias of the presentation which favored the British at the expense of the Americans. Part of this is due to the fact that Montgomery was hot with the newspaper reporters at the time, and was first in print with a history of the strategy, etc. But the later versions are probably more objective, and if you ponder the undeniable facts, it was probably Eisenhower who was able to put together the winning strategy, taking advantage of the changes in situation as they developed. This is not clear in this version, which gives as much space to the Free Polish Army as to the Americans.

At 3:15 we watched the movie (English version). The contemporary film clips are interesting – and it is interesting to guess how many of these are true action shots — and which are from training exercises, etc. Surely the daylight paratroop drops were not filmed in action, etc. It lasted 20 minutes, but you can't learn that much about it in that length of time. But the Battle of Normandy, and the Battle of the Bulge were the two most important on Western Front in WWII, and the Americans won them (not without the Allies, of course).

When we left, we figured out how to get to the road to Port-en-Bessin, and got there with only one small mis-step, namely driving down one wrong street out of the traffic circle, but this was repaired in 50 yards, so we drove back. We decided to go see Ponte de Hoc, since it was only 4 o'clock. This is the last stop on the Circuit des Debarquements and about 7 miles or so from Port-en-Bessin, 2 or 3 beyond the American Cemetery. It was a gun emplacement captured by the Rangers on D-Day, positioned so the 155 mm guns there could hit any target on Omaha or Utah beach. 280 Rangers scaled the cliffs, and knocked out the guns, which had been moved ½ mile inland. After 2 days, when they were relieved, there were only 80 Rangers still effective. Then we came back, and after a little while went to supper. The sunset and ocean filling the harbor was great. Mary Ann had cod-fish, which she said was good. There was a lot more wind than the night before, so after a 10-minute walk we came home and went to bed.

September 7

We got up about 8 AM and went down and had continental breakfast. You get enough to eat, and I can skip lunch with no difficulty, but I am beginning to long for a handful of trail mix, etc. So we watched the tide come in from ground level. We had figured out our target, namely Le Mont-St.-Michel, and the route there during breakfast, even down to the strategy for circumference road at Bayeux, with which we were familiar. This time I could believe that the trip to Bayeux from Port-en-Bessin is shorter than my commute drive to school in the morning. (Yesterday it seemed like 30 or 40 miles.) Anyway, we drove along through the beautiful French countryside, which is prosperous and self-contained. The people seem glad to be alive, perhaps a little too engrossed with the church, but they relieve this with very good wine, very good food, and it doesn't look as if there is overpopulation.

We drove along, and before too long we got stuck in a zone where some men were working, and we sat behind a huge truck for perhaps 10 minutes while the cars came from the other direction. The sign said it was the gas company. Anyway, after a while the line began to move, and really, there were only two guys with brooms sweeping around an already-filled hole beside the road, and two signalmen. (If it had never happened to us in the US, or even in GA, I would have more right to complain, but last year some time we were stuck in a worse case, going around Atlanta to the north.)

Anyway, before too long, we got tricked by a road sign again, made an incorrect 5 minute detour, then got on the sometimes dual, sometimes

Mont Saint-Michel

not, with the big green sign pointing to Le Mont-St.-Michel. As we approached Avranches there were some Scenic View signs, and a picnic area, and Mary Ann looked, and there was Le Mont-St.-Michel on the horizon. When she told me, I was able to sneak a quick look, abandoning momentarily the tail-gate sentry duty that seems to be prudent while driving here. Anyway, after 20 minutes or so we were approaching the right turn-off to Le Mont-St.-Michel, and the very helpful large green sign was on the left, and very shortly (100 yards later) was on the right, and I signaled a turn, but if I'd made it we'd have been smooshed, so there we were barreling along the dual lane with no place to turn around. So we went 2 or 3 miles, and were able to reverse our direction, in some small town, but there I couldn't figure it out going the other way. So we went 2 or 3 miles past in that direction, and reversed yet again, and finally made the turn. Needless to say, one's disposition does not improve during this exercise. So then we went along for 15 minutes, discussing various strategies for obtaining a room. There are 100s of "Chambre," "Chambre en ferme"s...even some motels, in the immediate neighborhood of Le Mont-St.-Michel, but somehow that didn't seem to be what we wanted, so we kept going, and then we were on the causeway. Le Mont-St.-Michel was 2+/- mi. away, very beautiful, but there were solid cars parked on the right side, as far as you could see. 100s, perhaps even 1000s, if you count those down below that were going to be underwater at 8:00 PM. But suddenly someone up ahead indicated he was leaving, and I grabbed it, even to the extent of backing in. Every time I back the car I congratulate myself for having learned how to get it in REVERSE. It was nice and windy, a little cloudy overhead, but raincoats were indicated for warmth, if for no other reason.

I wasn't the best dressed person at Le Mont-St.-Michel, but pilgrims come in all shapes and sizes, and during the course of the day I did see 2 or 3 other raincoats (on geriatrics). *De rigeur* is a windbreaker, anorak...

There were thousands of people, maybe we saw 5000, milling around like halftime at Sanford Stadium in an area ¼ the size. We arrived at the door of the Tourist Bureau on the dot of 12 (closing), back at 2, so we took off through the mob, up through the souvenir shops and bars and restaurants and sandwich shops and tea rooms. Before long we came to Thenice's house, for which we had free tickets sent in a huge book by the French Tourist Agency in New York City. We saved 30 F (or more), and we went into the house which was nice, 11th century, built by a knight, for his wife, as a safe house when he went off to lay siege to someone else's castle. The furniture was very fine, and there were 3 rooms, one on top of the other, and some nice little gardens. They had a suit of armor (5-foot men) and a model of Thenise (probably better looking than she was, but who knows?) sitting by a spinning wheel. We climbed up to the top floor, and were able to leave by a gate in the garden, which was the size of a motel room. So then we were at the foot of the abbey, and we looked at the view, went in and bought a book and some postcards, and discarded the idea of several possible children's gifts, and I got a notebook to finish the journal in.

We waited around for the next English speaking tour, ½ hour, got the elderly rate for tickets. The tour was good; the guide prided himself in his exposition. His blurb was written by a scholar, but there were a lot of jokes, and it is not obvious whose those were. The talk was simultaneously high and low level, and in between, so I was impressed. He explained the architectural details of structure, where the weight was supported, and the various principles of architecture, first appearing in cathedrals (high level), and how much wine each monk consumed (low level), etc. When we finished the tour it was 2:30, so, since I wasn't hungry, we passed up the restaurants, bistros, tea rooms, sandwich shops, bars,...went back to the Tourist Bureau. The lady there couldn't help us get a room elsewhere (reasonable, in that zoo), and we had no desire to stay in Le Mont-St.-Michel (How would you get your luggage in? etc). So we decided to join the pilgrims streaming out toward our car, and plied our way, turning around now and then to impress the different aspects of this beautiful place well in our minds. It is easy to see why, in 1100, it was decided to put a good church there.

At 3:00 we decided to try for Mortain, where Mary Ann's brother, Bob, fought during the war. We had studied the maps, the signs were easy, and by 4:00 we were parked on the main street, not too far from a bank, the post office, and an OK looking hotel. Mary Ann went to the Post Office, but the lady there had to have a weighing before she could give the cost of a stamp, and so Mary Ann went back to the car for a postcard. So we bought a lifetime supply of postcard stamps, got out

$300 in Francs for the weekend, and went across the street to the Hotel des Postes.

The girl at the desk was very pretty, 18+/-, and offered us a room at 275 F, but I said no, and so she said 170 F, and we went up and looked at it, and it was (is) nice (small bathroom, with a shower). In our room there was some blurb about Mortain (a large tennis complex, and swimming, and 2 cascades, large and small). I was glancing at this when I saw that there was a Memorial for the Soldiers of WWII. We decided to try to see it. It is at the Petite Chapelle, which we located on the map. We decided we couldn't walk that far. So we got in the car, and after some false turns (all my doing) we found the road to the Chapelle. We got to the parking lot for the Chapelle, and ignored the sign that said the grounds were open only to the pious, and walked along the ridge, in the middle of a forest about ¼ mile, and we came to the brand new black marble cross, with the insignia of Bob's division (I/30-OLD HICKORY) on it. Nearby is the Chapelle, which looks old (100 yrs.+/-). We explored around back, and there were steps up to a table sized circular stone. On top of this there was a beautiful ceramic map showing all of the places you could see from there, which had been placed there in 1913 by the Automobile Club of France. We were able to see Le Mont-St.-Michel, a little speck on the horizon. It was beautiful there, and truly, it is obvious why such a spot would be a necessity in a battle. Whoever was there could track everything that went on for at least 10 miles in every direction. We were both very pleased that we had found this spot, without really knowing it was there. We next met groups of elderly French citizens on the way back, and some boys on bicycles were playing there (but nicely). Then we drove to find a Grande Cascade, which was about 1 mile from our hotel, a small waterfall, but very nice to have in a city park.

September 8

We got up about 8:00. Then we went across the street to view the Town Hall, where formerly there was a plaque to the 30th Division, but we couldn't find it. Mary Ann took a photograph or two, and we walked down past the Saturday market, where the farm people were selling produce, nice fruit and vegetables, by the side of the street. We found a postcard with the memorial by the small chapel, so we were saved a trip up the hill to photograph it for her brother. We went to the Post Office to wing off a postcard. Then in the car across the countryside, along the ridge of the encirclement, almost certainly, and through the gently rolling, subtly changing country from boscage to open, which became the corridor of the break out.

Château d'Angers

We went through Domfront, around Mayenne, finally in Brittany, and then we reached our goal, Angers. We drove into Angers, parked in a big lot just across from the Tourist Bureau, in the shadow of the castle.

The castle at Angers houses the Apocalypse Tapestry. This is a monumental tapestry from the 12th century+/-, that wasn't completely saved, but perhaps ¾ of it was saved. The predictions of doom and allegory of fighting the devil were an important motivation for the founding of the early church, just as predictions of doom are necessary today. (Overpopulation <u>will</u> ruin the earth, oil <u>can</u> run out, etc.)

We left the tapestry and looked over the battlements. There was a family behind us with two daughters, 2 and 5+/-, and the 5-year-old climbed up on the battlement with a 150 ft. drop below, but the father did not seem too concerned. It frightened me. Then we walked down into the old town, down a barren alley, and came out at the square of the cathedral, and we looked for the famous door, which is being repaired, and badly in need of it, several of the figures having big chunks knocked out of them.

In Angers, we went to dinner. It was a very pleasant moonlit night. The streets were very nearly empty, except for a couple, and some bunches of 4 or 5 teenagers, having a good time, but behaving+/-. We ended up on the main street, and there was a band concert finishing up on the park across the street. We were 2 or 3 blocks from the hotel, and when we got there, there was a large military band in the last stages of preparing to march out. They had brass helmets, and very handsome uniforms, there must have been 60 members of the band. We waited on the corner, about 5 minutes, and off they went, playing a very nice march. Our patron was there watching, and he told us the band was from Paris, in town for a festival. So we went to bed.

September 9

We got up, went down to the small dining room for our continental breakfast, hopped in the Renault, and off toward Loches, without a reservation. The traffic was very light, being Sunday morning, and soon we were crossing the countryside with the Loire to our left, through towns with chateaux on the sides of the hill (Saumur, e.g.)

We were making very good time, and Mary Ann was reading the guidebook, telling me all of the things we were missing, so when she read about Fontevrauet-l'Abbe, and the fact that the Plantagenets were buried there, it seemed like a good chance. We glanced in the church, and followed the path to the Abbey, and we were exactly where we had started on our search for the Abbey, only this time we looked at the gate in front of our eyes, and there was the entrance. We crossed a gravel courtyard, and entered the room marked Billets, where there were postcards, guidebooks, etc., on sale, and there were 3 ladies keeping the shop, one of whom spoke English colloquially. She told us that the English language tour started in 3 minutes, so we stood around in the courtyard for 6-8 minutes, and our guide appeared, There were 10-12 people in our little throng, and she led us about 30 ft., into the kitchen, and sat us on some benches. After having asked us where we were from, 4 Americans, 6 British, an expatriate American from Naples, and his wife (+/-). The guide was a young Belgian lady. She was a sort of round girl, not too attractive, but enthusiastic, and she worked hard to dish up what we wanted. There were probably 5 books in the shop that contained the information she was telling, but it is fun to have the lecture illustrated by the stones in the wall right there. There were places where current construction allowed you to see the 11th century building overlaid by the 15th century building overlaid by the 19th, and if you really needed it, a telephone.

As the talk went on, our guide lapsed into her own reconstruction of history, some of which was blatant nonsense (like Richard the Lionhearted being a bad guy). At the end of the tour, there were tombs of Richard the Lionhearted, Eleanor of Aquitaine, Henry I of France, and Anne of Brittany. During the Revolution, the stone statues were removed and hidden by the nuns, and so they were saved, but they were separated from the royal bones, and there is an archeological project in progress, to try to locate them. There was one skull just barely visible in an open trench. It looked as if it had been placed so adults could see it, but children could not.

We hopped in our car, abandoned the Loire, and went cross-lots through Chinon, to Loches. We went back down the hill, to the Hotel de Ville, which was opposite the Tourist Bureau. The girl minding the bar, which doubled as the reception, showed us a room that was nice, and we checked in.

The castle at Loches is known as the place where Joan of Arc came for the second time to see the king, Charles VII, to ask him to go and be crowned in Rhiems. They had a book with a record of her trial. The walls surrounded an area of several acres, and the chateau had a few nice things – a painting of the King's mistress, Agnes Sorel, and some armor and weapons. We skipped the torture chamber. There was a small temporary display of uniforms, WWI and WWII, with some insignia and medals, etc. These were in 2 rooms in the Tower, and you had to climb up narrow, circular staircases to get there. From the top we were able to get out on the battlements, where we could see the hotel we couldn't get in, and the town, and into a room where two girls were having tea.

Castle at Loches

We walked down off the ramparts into the old town, and a 10-year-old boy ran past us with an ice cream cone, and went in the gate to a very nice house, through a courtyard the size of a motel room. After dinner we took a moonlight tour of the old town. The chateaux at night are impressive, and the floodlights are turned on to help tourism, and on a perfect September night one can feast his eyes on other-world conceits.

September 10

We slipped down and had our continental breakfast served by the patron, walked across the street to see if the Tourist Bureau was open (closed Monday), and we saw all of the mothers and fathers taking their children to a school not far away. The ones we saw drive, find a parking space, all get out and march off to school, to arrive at 9:00 I suppose. Not too different from Athens, except we didn't see any school buses.

Commune at Chenonceaux

Then we checked out, off to Chenonceaux. It was not too far, 25 min.+/-, and before too long the road signs for Chenonceaux appeared. We were going cross-lots, with almost no traffic, but as we came into the neighborhood, there began to be some tour buses. We parked our little car, and walked 100 ft. to the Billets, and off through the gates.

Chenonceaux is privately owned and operated, by the family of a chocolate manufacturer, and things were run better there. The antiques were more authentic, better cared for, and the room restoration more alive. In some sense, there was a great similarity in the tourist provisions everywhere, the same books for sale, the same postcards and souvenirs.

At any rate, I had a stamp with Chenonceaux on it, and the idea of a castle over a river intrigued me.

Finally toward the end of the tour through the chateau there was an exhibit of modern art, paintings by Pierre Boncampain. The exhibition was housed in the upper gallery, the width of the river. There were 50+/- large paintings, and I liked them a lot. The first bunch seemed on beyond Matisse, color patterns, with people. But then there were landscapes, with soft colors, and nudes, and still lifes, all more modern than others I have seen. The pictures were for sale, the exhibit arranged by a Paris art dealer. The girl at the disk of the exhibit was very fashionably dressed, with a black Spanish hat, and a nice smile.

We looked at a couple more rooms, went outside, bought some postcards, and sat on the edge of the garden and looked at the castle for 15 or 20 minutes, back to our car, and off to Chambord.

We left around noon, and went on secondary roads, for a little way along the Cher, then left at Montrichard, through huge vineyards to Bracieux and finally through a forest, until we came to the gate of the park of Chambord, and then after 2 or 3 miles, we could see the chateau. So we followed the PARKING signs, and were able to park ¼ mile down the road, and walked back. There was a hotel right there, and we were able to get a room (next door to the WC), in a building that had been used for the servants when the castle was being used. The castle was used as a hunting lodge on several occasions by Louis XIV, and the first

Castle at Chambord

performance of a play by Moliere ("The Counterfeit Gentleman"), was performed in one of the rooms on the 1st floor. We were both tired, and a little hungry, and *two major castles are too much in one day*, but we stood on the balcony and watched 3 men with horses in 16th century costume parade across the lawn, advertising the horsemanship show to take place at 5:30.

We went down to dinner at 7:45. After dinner we walked around the outside of the castle for ½ hour or so, looking at it from all angles, reflected in the moat. The floodlights were on, and it is beautiful at night, with the weathering of the stones muted, and the shadows from the lights throwing it all into a picture book perspective.

Chartres Cathedral

September 11

We got up a little after 8, went downstairs for our breakfast, and after a lengthy wait, were served. By the time we were served there were 20 or so people waiting, some more patiently than others. We ate, checked out, and off to Chartres. This involved going through Blois, and at a critical traffic circle we missed the turn, so we had to turn around, and there was a lot of traffic, and you had to know you were going to Chartres and on through several traffic circles. Finally, after a long ride through huge wheat fields, numerous towns, etc., we arrived at Chartres. You can see the two spires of the cathedral 6 or 8 miles from town, straight down the road.

We went about 100 ft. farther, passing teenage students who had just been released, and went in the cathedral. It is the 3rd largest cathedral, and is impressive. But the windows are far, far away, and even though there is a lot of help so you can follow the stories in them, if you want to, you can't see the detail. I was impressed by the fact that cleaning a window costs many thousands of dollars, so only a few have been cleaned in the last 10 years, and some of the dirty ones are very dirty. I wandered the length of the church, which contains numerous chapels, and much sculpture and wood carving, but was unable to add these things to the too much I had seen already. We hopped in our car, and off to Versailles.

We found the Tourist Bureau, and one of the young ladies accepted our case. She called the Tourist Bureau in Paris, and there was nothing in all of Paris. Apparently this was the week of education meetings, or something. But finally, she called back to Ramboullet, and got us in a room, at the St. Charles. Ramboullet was back down the road about 8 or 10 miles. It was about 50 ft. from the first gate of an ancient military school (artillery), which is still very much in use. So we drove up to the gate, turned around, and back through a narrow passage into their parking. We went in, and got our room, which was nice, and rested for awhile, until it was time for dinner. The patronne was a lady about 40-years-old, and she wouldn't recommend a restaurant. No one in France ever recommended a restaurant. Once or twice someone said "A restaurant exists at this point," but never was there a recommendation. Anyway, we went back to town in search of the Restaurant de Postes, described in our guidebook. We parked in the church lot, walked down the hill after asking directions from a well-dressed man who spoke English. Anyway, he told us the wrong way, and after walking 3 or 4 blocks we asked a young man (probably a soldier) who was walking in the direction we wanted to go. He offered the information that the best restaurant in town was across the street from Rest. De Postes (Ignore the previous remark about no one giving us a recommendation.). So we checked the menu, and it was 10 F more expensive, so we went to the Rest. De Postes. While we were eating several more parties came in, perhaps 20 more people, and just as we were leaving another bunch came in. Then we went back to the St. Charles, and went to bed.

September 12

We got up, and went down and had our continental breakfast, and on the advice of our patron, decided to take the train to Paris. There was an English couple who gave us the needed instructions on how to get from the train to the Metro. So we walked the mile or so up to the train station, and got there about 9:15 and had to wait for 15 minutes or more while the train came. We were the second on the platform, but by the time the train came there were 20 or 30 people waiting – students, businessmen, elderly ladies, a man with two children, secretaries,...We got seats, separated, at first, and off we went on the Direct. They don't take tickets, but the penalties are severe if you don't have one.

We didn't really have a goal, but I wanted to see the Picasso Museum, so we aimed for that first. We couldn't figure out the last stage of the Metro (we wasted 10 or 15 minutes trying to do it), so we surfaced at the Place de Bastille and walked the 4 or 5 blocks to the museum. It was a beautiful September morning, and the people walking in Paris seemed to be enjoying themselves. The museum is in a big old house, sort of back in, but we located it after a while, and it is a good museum, but not so good as the one on Barcelona. There are some fine things, the Blue Period old woman with the cast eye, Paul as Pierette, a different two-faced one of Marie-Therise than you usually see, the man carrying the goat, etc. In addition, there was a room full of ones he had traded for, Rousseau, Braque, Matisse,...

I had been just totally crammed full of new museum-type things, and didn't care if I saw any more, but the Picasso was like coming home. I saw lots of new things, but I knew where they fit.

We took a quick tour of the garden, and Mary Ann didn't want to have anything to eat, so we decided to walk down to the Seine. The traffic on the streets we walked down was barely moving. There weren't any parking spaces. After a 10 minute walk we were down by the river, and we saw a sign for the boat ride, and after making our way around some construction we got onto the boat just as it was about to leave. We chugged down the river to the Eiffel Tower, but decided to stay on. Mary

River Seine with Eiffel Tower in the background

Ann wanted to see the Musee d'Orsay, which has the Impressionists, and their ilk. So we got off, and walked over and under some very busy streets and soon were at the museum. The museum is a book in itself; we walked its length, bought a guidebook, and went back to Ramboullet. On the train ride back there was a couple opposite us, and she had been to the doctor and had a long letter, handwritten, with his diagnosis, which she was reading. The train was a double-decker, we were on the upper deck. It was full, but no one had to stand. So after 6 or 7 stops, while the commuters disembarked, we came slowly to our stop. We retraced ourselves, with the help of the map on the back of the card from St. Charles, pausing to photograph the telephone sculpted in boxwoods in the city park. We looked at all of the menus in the restaurants as we passed, and they were all too expensive, but not so elegant as the one in which we had eaten the night before.

We drove up the hill again, parked in the church lot, and made our way to the Cheval Rouge, the restaurant recommended by the young man the night before.

It was slightly better...AND slightly more pretentious. There was a party of diplomats at a large table in the next room — French, English, and an Arab, and they spoke in English, and they were talking some about the mid-east crisis, and some of it was just ordinary conversation. There were 2 Germans at another table. When we finished we wended our way back, and to bed.

September 13

We woke up early – even though it wasn't too far, we figured we would need 2 or 3 hours to get to Orly. We were going cross lots, via Chevreuse. Someone was up before we were, so I didn't feel too bad, but at 7:30 or so, I got the patronne to the desk, in her bathrobe, to pay the bill. I asked for directions to Chevreuse, and it's just as well I did, because we wouldn't have gone that way.

So we left town by a road that went by the train station, and after 2 or 3 miles came to a rotary we couldn't figure out. After abandoning the correct road, trying another which dissipated in a subdivision, and back, losing 15 minutes, we were trundling down the road, from small town to small town, on the midst of parents taking children to school and people going to work. We finally, using 3 maps, found a formula for making progress, until we hit the main road. The cars were bumper to bumper, trucks impossible to see over to read the signs, with no chance to switch into a proper lane if you weren't there. But after a while we saw signs to Orly, and then we had to be sharp, to distinguish Orly (the town) from Orly (the airport). We got in the airport finally, but still didn't know how to return our car. So we made a tour of the lane for departing planes. Mary Ann got out and asked a policeman, then the guy at Europacar, who directed us, more or less, to the point for returning cars.

Dear Older Me,

This is a short account of an incident which happened on another trip to France, this time in the southern portion of the country. It was a wonderful trip, full of resplendent vistas and multiple educational opportunities for my LLLP. We saw some of the remnants of Caesar's Gallic Wars and the Roman occupation of Gaul. We considered buying oranges in Orange, but thought better of it. We took a bullet train from Paris to Avignon and visited the Pope's Palace (1309-early 1400s). We danced on the bridge at Avignon. We saw some young men swimming with a dolphin in the sea off Colliure. But, far and away my most poignant memory of that trip was being robbed by a family of gypsies well-schooled in their art, in Arles.

October 11

We arose, about 8:30, and went down to breakfast, this time in the bar, since the other room was full of the tour, 15+/- Germans, eagerly waiting for the next stage. We consumed the 3 rolls dished up, the coffee and the chocolate, and then it was 9:00 and I was off to the bank. After consultation with the boy at the desk I decided to walk rather than drive, even though it was drizzling. When I got there, the door was mysterious, but in a moment a man off to the side motioned me in, but the floor was completely torn up, and a man was working on it, and he motioned for me to a 1 foot patch on the side, and when I got to the Titres window I paused, looking for my next move and the true functionaire said, alertly, to stay there, to not go on to Change. Then the jerk made me wait the symbolic French minute and a half while he pretended that he was doing something. We smoothly exchanged $400, at 5.62+/- and I walked back to the hotel under the careful scrutiny of several people who had watched my progress in the other direction...

October 14, 1991

Statement to the Police:

I am Dr. Thomas Brahana, Professor Emeritus of the University of Georgia, Athens, Georgia, USA. My wife and I are on vacation in France. The last 3 nights we stayed in Avignon, at the Hotel Mignon, Rue Jules Verne. This morning we drove to Arles, and arrived at 10:30 AM. We parked our car near Rue Marius Jouveau, in the parking area near the levee. We walked up to the Arena and 3 individuals asked us for money, possibly in exchange for some printed material. These 3 individuals were, first, a young girl (age 8-10), second, a young man, and third, a woman (possibly 40 years old). They asked several times for money, and I shook my head. The young man jostled my wife, and the woman touched me.

The money that was taken from me was contained in a blue American Express plastic folder. I had placed it in my left hand pants pocket, after getting out of the car. (My wife had it in her purse, while I was driving.) We were not near any person in going from the car to the sidewalk near the arena. My blue plastic folder contained approximately 1400 F, in denomination:

1—500 F

4—200 F

2—50 F

(This may not be precise, although the amount is close to correct.)

In addition there was $1300 in American Express Travelers Checks.

My wife spoke to me during this incident, and immediately I felt in my pocket, and realized that my money had been taken. The boy was still beside me, and I raised a cry for the police.

He went off down a side street, and I remained with him for perhaps 100-200 yards, I did not leave sight of him, nor was he more than 2 meters distant from me, until we were met by 3 or 4 police officers. I did not touch him.

The officers instructed me to come to the Prefecture of Police at 14:00.

This incident is the basis for my complaint.

Thomas Brahana

163 S. Homewood Dr.

Athens, GA. 30606

Arles

OUR PLAN WAS TO DRIVE SOUTH, TO ARLES, AND SEE THE CAMARGUE, WHICH IS NAME FOR THE DELTA OF THE RHONE. The deltas of the world produce much of the food, and each has its own character. We changed some money, and walked to the tourist place in the Gare, to make a reservation in Arles. We drove along through the Monday morning traffic, and the road was not extremely busy, but there were some trucks rolling along, ready to make you extinct if you make a wrong move. After a pleasant drive of an hour or so, we arrived at Arles, and parked by the quai', and made our way toward the arena. The last bullfight of the season had been held there the day before. The street circling the arena was crowded with traffic, say 100 people and 20 cars and trucks.

As we walked up the hill we were approached by gypsies, 2 children and a woman, asking for charity. They pushed papers at us, and the woman brushed my shoulder and picked my pocket, stealing 1500 F, and $1400 in traveler's checks. The young teenager pushed against Mary Ann, and she said (more alert than I), "Tom, your money!" I felt in my pocket, knew it had been taken, and jumped over next to the boy, and called for the police, yelling. He ran away, but I stayed with him, making a terrible noise. He offered to let me search him, but I said, "No, no." Within two minutes, the police were there, 4 of them, in a car. I told them what had happened, and they asked, "Do you wish to make a complaint?" I said, "Yes," and they said, "Go to the Prefecture at 2:00." They took the boy off in their car. So, non-trivially agitated, we located the Tourist Bureau, found our hotel, The Cloister, on Rue de Cloitre, looking into the 15th century Cloister, one of the top tourist attractions in Arles. So I spent my noon hour writing an account of what had happened, for my interview at 2:00. I went to the sub-prefecture, and was directed to the Hotel de Police, about 3 blocks away on the main avenue in Arles.

When we got there, we were asked to wait on a bench, and after about 3 minutes were led upstairs to be interviewed by a youngish inspector (30+/-), rather handsome, dressed in informal street clothes (a sweater, jeans perhaps). He called for his colleague, and they showed me photographs of 3 young girls, in gypsy costumes, and asked if I could identify the youngster. The first was too old, and the third was not the one. I studied the middle one, and perhaps imprudently, said, "That's the one." She was the right age, and had the same general appearance, but I had at most a 30 second glance, so I should have been more cautious.

The scene is very sharp in my memory, even now. The colleague was Inspector Brigette Rodriguez, a slightly older lady, who was there to translate. She read from my account, as the young man filled out the form. They asked very pointedly, "Was it the children who had taken the money?" I said "No, no. It was the woman." We were in the room perhaps 10 minutes or so, the inspector had taped the complaint, I read it, and signed it. Mme. Rodriguez told me to call today or tomorrow to learn if they had apprehended the woman, and I asked her to write her name on the card, since I couldn't do French on the phone, which she did.

That is my account of an experience many American tourists to France have experienced, the fabled "Gypsy Handshake," one of the more expensive handshakes on the planet, ranking right up there with the political fundraiser handshake and the Ponzi scheme handshake.

WALES & IRELAND

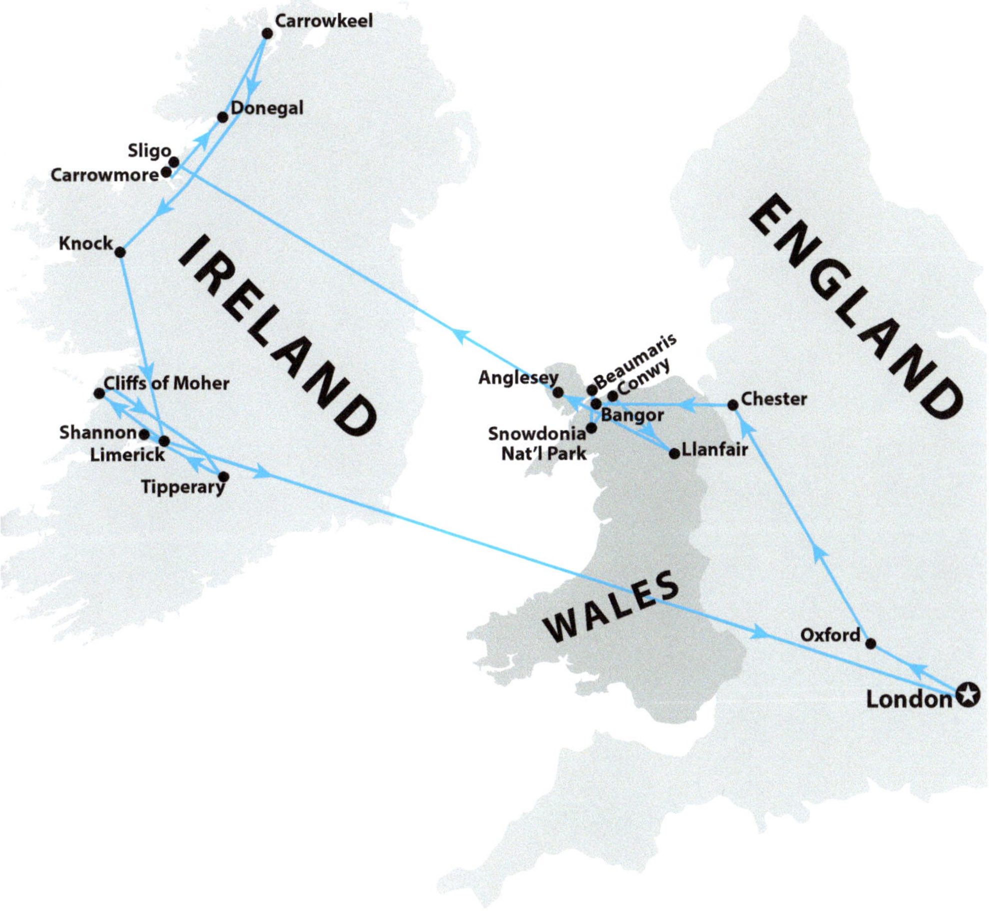

Wales is both a part of Britain and entirely its own culture. Remnants of Edward I's subjugation are still evident to this day. The Welsh have strong agricultural and manufacturing traditions. Music is a large part of their identity. The Welsh language is unique and one of the most difficult on the planet to learn.

July 4, 1994

WE ARE ENROLLED IN AN ELDERHOSTEL, OUR FIRST. This morning at 9 o'clock Rusty came to Athens to take us to the airport, in a light drizzle, which promises to be heavier later, due to a storm moving up from the Gulf. We got to the airport (Hartsfield) with 3 hrs. to spare, and the airport is not very busy. The biggest change from last year in the airport is the large TV screen playing CNN news continuously. I am not certain that I like this. We were eventually called to board for our Atlantic crossing. The plane was filled, at least in Tourist Class.

July 5

At about 6:00 we were spit out into Heathrow, along with 2000 other people.

We arrived and filed out into a beautiful sun-lit morning to await pick-up by the 27-seat Marriott bus. We checked in our room, and decided to go sight-seeing in England. It was still only 8:00 AM. We got our directions to Oxford. Our trip, through lake country, was interesting, but not as interesting as Oxford itself. There we toured England's smallest cathedral, built near the remnants of an 8th century church. Their collection was small, but there was an excellent portrait of Cardinal Wolsey, Oxford's benefactor until he failed to secure a divorce for Henry VIII. Then back to the Elderhostel.

After a nap, we attended our initial Elderhostel briefing, and walked in to a room of 36+/- icy elderly glances. We went to dinner, Beef Bourguignon and potatoes, roll and ice cream, coffee. After dinner I did my exercise routine in the weight room, came to the room, and went to bed.

July 6

We woke up about 6:30 for a 7:00 breakfast call, and the breakfast was indeed a display of all the things that humans have started their days with. We talked to an oriental lady, a classmate, who grilled us about former President Jimmy Carter. She was a librarian and this is her first Elderhostel. She quickly got to the heart of things, with oriental directness, and asked if we liked Jimmy or not, and if we liked Rosalyn or not, and similar soul-searching probes. Her husband didn't offer much, except, "I think they should serve breakfast all day."

Our next excursion was to Bangor, but we stopped at Chester along the way. The EH lecture of the day was heavy on WWII, including visiting a monument to the Welsh RAF fighters in the war.

Bangor

We went into Bangor, a town of 15,000+/-, and up Love Lane about 100 yards, before coming to our dormitory. We de-bused and were taken into the bar for briefing, given our room assignments, and told that we would eat at 6:30, in maybe an hour. We went for a short walk, went back to the bar at about 6:15 and joined a small group having cocktails, and we each had a beer. Then it was dinner time. Our local coordinator, Kathryn, sat next to me. She is from a Welsh town about 20 miles away, and she learned to speak Welsh before English;

she is a nice bubbly girl in her 2nd year at college, and when I asked her would she like to go back to her village when she finishes school she did not know what to say, so she endorsed my suggested, "see what turns up." Being a younger person to talk to, she fills a badly needed gap in the Edlerhostel program. After supper we took a walk in the immediate neighborhood.

July 7

We got up and took a twenty minute walk around the neighborhood, locating the adjacent banks, drugstores, etc. Then we had breakfast, and after a little break, off to class. Our lecturer is Cledwin Jones, a professor of continuing education here. The University of Wales requires that you speak Welsh in order to enter, which was Cledwin's native tongue. His subject fits in with autobiographical digression, in which he indulges. The chairs are Spartan, and the sessions are long. So, as always, a teacher must answer questions in a way that discourages irrelevant inquiry. After our lecture we had lunch.

In the afternoon we took the bus to town, in which we were given an hour to explore, and then off to Beaumaris. We went into the castle, and saw an unfinished, well-designed example from a string of medieval fortifications, commissioned by Edward I (late 13th century).

Castle at Beaumaris

We came back and attended a concert by the Bangor Male Voice Choir. They started with a Beethoven, and then Mozart, "Isis and Osiris," and then a number of Welsh songs, some Negro Spirituals, and a couple of hymns. The concert was well received by our group, who were the only audience. Male voice choirs are a strong tradition in Wales, dating back to the slate mining and coal mining days, when the men sang as they went to work, and in the mines. The singers were middle-aged, for the most part, and have been together 6½ years, and are beginning to tour, record, etc. We learned the next morning that the choir stayed in our bar for two or three hours, drinking and singing. After the concert we went to bed, in our separate rooms.

July 8

We got up a little early and went on a short walk before breakfast, to the conjectured nearby spot of the Roman camp, that may or may not have been the location of an outpost of the legions. There are no visible signs of the Romans.

We had breakfast, and then class, in which Mr. Jones more or less followed the schedule. He used the pedagogical ploy, "You are a very good class, but..." once, and I was surprised at the time because it was several minutes from the "You are a very good class" part to the "but..." part and I kept waiting for the shoe to drop. When it did he overlaid it in so much circumlocution that I almost missed it. (The "but" part was "if you keep asking so many stupid questions I won't be able to keep to the schedule," stated much more diplomatically of course.) We got a condensed version of the Conquest of Wales by Edward I.

At Caernarvon, we toured a slate mine, with a tour mainly devoted to detailing the harsh mine conditions: 12 hour shifts in candle-lit dank conditions and other horrors from a modern perspective. When we got home we went to bed.

Snowdonia National Park

July 9

We got up a little later, no walk before breakfast. After a decent interval, we loaded onto the bus for a tour of the National Park of Snowdonia. I am not certain of the status of national parks in the UK, but the visible aspect here is regional planning to provide for multi-faceted land use – in particular, sheep (and to a lesser extent cattle) farming, forestry, hydro-electric power, and especially recreation: rock climbing, trail hiking, camping, fishing, biking, picnicking, etc.

Welsh wool was manufactured (carded, and woven) in this area, and occasionally blended with wool from New Zealand. Then home, and to bed.

July 10

We got up a little after 7:00 and ate breakfast, and then we took a longish walk to the Telford Bridge. It was on the edge of raining, and we walked about a mile along the road with the cars buzzing by. There was a path above the road, built in celebration of the coronation of Queen Elizabeth II. The rain and mist cut down the visibility, and we decided to go back, and we arrived in time for lunch.

After lunch we had a trip to Conwy Castle, another in the string of Edward's fortifications. The whole trip was directed by young Katheryn, who showed us the mountain atop of which her music teacher, a retired opera star, had a house. The castle was part of the wall of the town, and there was an access from the sea, which now is blocked by another bridge by Telford. After a while we meandered down to the bus, in the midst of our colleagues, whom we are now getting to know better.

Our main lecturer, Cledwin Jones, at one point gave us a short speech on "If you've seen one of Edward's castles, you've seen them all." There is some validity in this remark. We retraced our trip from Conwy to Bangor, and had roast Yorkshire Pudding.

Our entertainment for the evening was a harpist, Elinor Bennett. We learned later that her husband is the local MP. She began by explaining that she had just purchased her harp, which is 200-years-old, and a single stringed instrument as opposed to modern instruments, which are double or triple.

This was the first concert in which Elinor had played this instrument, which she had located through a well-known dealer in historic instruments. She had just finished re-stringing it with thinner strings, closer to its original configuration. Her first selection was "Variations on a Theme" by Mozart. She played mainly music from the period of the instrument, and numerous Welsh songs. Ms. Bennett is a professor at the university, and probably one of the best harpists playing now. She has large, strong hands, and a very gracious lecturing manner. I thoroughly enjoyed the information she was laying on us. I could sense that she was becoming acquainted with the instrument. The harp is the best instrument, or one of the best, with which to start understanding counterpoint. There aren't a lot of extra sounds imposed – just the two melodic lines. Her concert was well-received by our crew. After the concert we went to bed, at 10:00+/-.

July 11

We had our good dorm breakfast, with an orange from Israel. The class was about the Industrial Revolution in Wales, and Mr. Jones talked some about the men from Bangor who were industrialists, mainly from slate and shipping, and the need for slate for the houses of the workers. Mr. Jones grew up in a slate mining town, and clearly his sympathies were with the workers, and their struggle for social benefits, a decent life. His admiration for Lloyd George is tinged with a little censure, perhaps, because of Lloyd George's womanizing, but there is no question that when he listed the various improvements pushed through by the Labor Party, that he considered these the important events of the period: child labor laws, widows' benefits, disability insurance, etc.

I skipped lunch, so I could catch the bus to Llanfair P.K., the village with the long name, from which I could walk to Bryn Cilli Dhu, which is about 4 mi. away. I had seen a photograph of this site in my studies, and visiting there was something high on my list of priorities. I used the local tour bus to find the road leading to a tomb I wanted to see.

I walked what seemed like a long way up to the crossroad and finally, there was the little sign pointing to Bryn Cilli Dhu, and a road with a gate and instructions that from there you have to walk. The tomb is visible from there, a grassy mound set in gently rolling fields, green, sheep grazing, a drainage stream on the side. The road approaches the grave.

There is a working farm right there, white washed buildings, the farming taking place to within 30 feet of the tomb, where there is a fence,

Interior room of the tomb at Bryn Cilli Dhu

and instructions to stay near the fence, on a sign near the sheep barrier. When I walked across the field, the sheep collected and went to the other end. I went in and circled the tomb, in the spirit of the instructions on the sign. The tomb has features of two main types of megalithic monuments, namely a passage grave as in Newgrange, and a massive dolmen and lintel, I suppose, opposite the passage in the inner room, over which is the dry wall, circular domed ceiling.

The stones of the dolmen and lintel must have been worked with considerable precision. There is a modern supporting beam behind the lintel, but it must be to keep the stones and soil of the roof from moving, rather than support for the massive stones. The room has a narrow window, opposite the passage. I think this was probably covered when the site was operational in megalithic times. It is oriented to sunrise at the Winter Solstice. Finally, my circular survey convinced me that visitors were regularly entering the tomb, the door gate was not locked, and there were tennis shoe prints in the passage, so I went in. The interior room was more or less the size of our dining room back home.

I didn't see any megalithic marks on the stones inside. After 5 or 10 minutes inside I went back out, circled the tomb again, looking at the 20-30 holes on the site where some very recent probes had been filled in. During all of my time at the site I didn't see anyone, only the sheep.

Across the road, school had just finished for the day, and six or eight mothers were loading their cars, and one or two mini-vans, as I walked by. I wondered what effect going to grammar school where you could look out the window and see one of the most celebrated megalithic monuments would have on a child.

I returned on the reverse route of my trip, arriving back at Bangor in plenty of time for dinner, tired from all of the walking. I took a shower and felt much better.

That night after supper, we had the dancers, Downoyr Mon, who performed for us, a number of set dances which originated in the area, Anglesey (Mon), and North Wales generally.

July 12

We got up, 7ish, ate breakfast, and went to our last class with Cledwyn. Cledwyn ran his classes as seminars, and fielded questions as they were posed. The first hour and a half dealt with Richard Price, a Welshman who was in contact with Benjamin Franklin and Thomas Jefferson at the time of the American Revolution. Price wrote a pamphlet in 1776, on Civil Liberty, which advocated American independence, and Cledwyn would have us believe that he was very influential. There were other pamphleteers. As a representative of the Welsh spirit, the independence of Welsh thought, their disinterested approach to politics...I am comfortable with Richard Price.

The final hour was devoted to Welsh music, and Cledwyn sang. The intertwining of music with the Welsh cultural heritage is interesting, and worth thinking about. After class I asked him if he was familiar with

Haydn's collection of Welsh folk songs and he said yes. Then we had lunch, a short nap, and loaded up for a trip to Angelsey.

Afterward we crossed the bridge, making the confusing turn to Beaumaris, where Cledwyn took us to the church. He was a friend of the priest, and there were several important archeological artifacts there – a stone sarcophagus, which had contained the coffin of Joan, the wife of Llewelyn I of Wales, discovered in use as a horse trough in the 1700s.

As we rode home we could see lots of gardens, roses in full bloom everywhere. The grass is lovely and green everywhere, due to the abundance of rain.

We arrived back at the dorm, ate dinner, and then went to our farewell party. The campus coordinator Kathryn, was a voice student at the university, and she sang several songs for us, Welsh folk songs, etc. She has a fine voice, full, with very good presence, and she is pretty. It was a successful party, everyone felt good, and afterwards we went to bed.

July 13

We got up and had breakfast, sharing the dining room with 10+/- visitors who were there for the graduation ceremonies. When we showed up the bus wouldn't start, and this naturally caused some excitement. After a while a local bus was hired to take us to Holyhead. We had our lunch on the patio outside the common room/bar in our dorm in Bangor. We drove across Anglesey, a flat, pleasant countryside. I know we must have come close to Parys, a mountain which in the 1800s produced a substantial portion of the world's copper.

Anglesey is one of the more fertile spots along the west coast of Wales and England. Its antiquities are complicated by its continuous occupation. After an hour or hour and a half we came into Holyhead, without seeing very much of the town, going straight to the ferry. We looked after our own things, moving them in carts from the bus to the hold. We walked on and grabbed seats on the upper deck, so we could watch the ship leave port.

There was a very nice view of Snowden from here, distinguishable as the highest peak in the range off to the east. There were probably 200 passengers on the ferry, day trippers mostly. We went in and had dinner in the cafeteria. The crossing was smooth, sunny and a little breezy, and several people were sunbathing on the top deck. The ferry was a pleasure cruiser, with gambling, bars, a dance floor with live entertainers, a duty free shop, etc.

We finally worked our way into St. Angela's, after having missed a turn or two. We were given coffee and a scone and our room assignments, and the information that this was the latest an Elderhostel bus had arrived there. We got our luggage in, and went to bed.

July 14

We got up, and went downstairs to breakfast at 8:00 sharp, and just inside of the dining room door were handed a bowl of porridge, enough for a week if you did not quickly prevent it. We went to class, and Martin Enwright introduced himself, as our lecturer. His degree was in archeology and history, and he shared the lecturing duties with his wife, Joyce, who is a licensed archeologist who excavates endangered sites, before the road-builders move in with their bulldozers and land scrapers. The Common Market has stringent laws about the impact of development on environmental/archeological sites to which they contribute, and as a result she has gotten in on the ground floor in an expanding industry. Martin himself is a middle school teacher, an ebullient man in his forties. He began his lectures with a general outline of the course, and a description of our course-related trips.

Megaliths at Carrowmore

Martin summarized the status of the development of archeology here pretty well. At any time there are numerous theories about how things were. Acceptance of them is slow and may or may not take place, depending on new finds, etc.

We went to lunch, above average dorm food and after an hour or so, piled on the bus for the afternoon trip. Our first stop was a holy spring, dedicated to St. Mary I suppose, which was almost certainly a sacred place in pre-Christian days. There are a large number of recent statues made of plaster, an altar for Mass. There is a day in the spring when the services are held. There was a little tree on which ailing persons had tied ribbons, in the hope that their illnesses would be cured. There were 35+/- ribbons fluttering, but I don't know how many cures had been obtained.

We hopped back on the bus, and drove through the outskirts of Sligo, to arrive in Carrowmore. We came to the interpretation site. The site has been recently worked by a Swedish team, and the boy showing us the video was probably a student who had been a laborer for them. Anyway, he was simultaneously arrogant and not well-informed, a bad combination.

After the video, our half of the bus went out for a 20 minute tour, giving us a chance to see a few stone circles and some dolmen tombs. My survey only confused me. The proximity of Knockmarea and Maeve's Tomb adds to the confusion. Was this a natural spot to begin farming?

We got back on the bus, wended our way back to St. Angela's, past the church Drumcliffe where Yeats is buried, with Martin's promise that we would stop another time. For dinner there was a very nice salmon, caught that morning, boned and served cold as appetizer, and ham, and vegetables, and apple pie. To me this was our best dinner at St. Angela's. The dining room was very pleasant, with large windows looking out on the garden toward the lake. After dinner we took a walk in the garden, and then to the common room for some Irish music and dance. An Irishman in his mid-forties introduced a group of young people, 2 girls and 2 boys. The elder boy, about 17, was the dancer, and the elder girl played the Irish pipe, which has two bags, one for each elbow, and no mouthpiece, and is not easy to play. The younger girl played the violin. The dancing is spirited, with the upper body rigid. I sat there looking at them closely, trying to figure out how they were related, and the elder girl seemed to have a look of my daughter Elizabeth.

Afterward I went to talk to the man, and eventually told him my family came from near Ballymote, and were Brehenys, and he said that his wife is a Breheny. Incredible. They performed for an hour so, a "Danny Boy," and others I know. The little boy, Michael, 11, played the penny whistle, and it wasn't clear he was going to perform, but he did and the EHers gave him a nice hand, which pleased him a lot. After the concert we walked around a little more, it was still light, and went to bed.

July 15

We got up 7ish and had breakfast at 8:00 sharp. Our breakfast drill was rather pleasant.

After breakfast, at 9:00 we went across the drive to our classroom, to Joyce's first lecture. She relied on the screens, her sequence of slides, and a diagrammatic chronology, taken from a book, by Michael Ryan, *The Illustrated Archeology of Ireland*, 1991. Three hours to cover 7000 years of pre-history and history means that no subject gets adequately examined. She couldn't even talk much about the slides which showed her at digs when she was a student.

We went to lunch, had a short nap, and there was an afternoon trip to Sligo.

We had to wait quite a while when we got to the bus, since one of our number had taken off by herself, without checking out with Katherine. After about 20 minutes, the bus left with the 36 of us.

We ate dinner, and then went for an (optional) boat ride on Lough Gil. We rode over to Parke's Castle, 5 mi. or so, on the bus, waited around for 5 minutes or so for the boatman, and then took a half hour ride up and down the lake, viewing the Lake Isle of Innesfree, hearing Yeats recited by the boatman, and getting a nice view of St. Angela's from the lake. The lake was a tiny bit choppy in the evening breeze, but not really. The son of the boatman, who was 12+/-, was the mate, bartender,...and the boatman offered a prize if you could quote Yeats – Catherine from Dublin could. I bought a Guinness, which I enjoyed. We retraced our steps, to St. Angela's and to bed.

July 16

This was the day of our long excursion to Donegal. We saw Ben

Bulben, the castle where Lord Montbatten was assassinated, lunched at an historical folk village, returned home, and wandered the woods and the lake outside our Elderhostel.

We went inside and went to bed.

July 17

We got up at 7:30 AM and had breakfast this Sunday. We took the church bus into town and wandered while the faithful worshipped.

We were working our way through town when we came to the taxi rank. So I decided to ask what the charge would be to take a taxi to the digs at Carrowkeel, and the man said, after a little thought, 25 pounds. I didn't have to think much about that, and I said goodbye to Sweet Mary Ann. (Had it not been for the necessity to tell the bus people not to wait, she could have come too.) The first driver put me back to the next one in line, and we were on our way. The driver, Chris Majors, is an Englishman who married a girl from a small town near Sligo. He lived in England until 10+/- years ago when he emigrated here. We talked full-speed all the time we were together, and I liked him as a person. Next was Lough Arrow, a beautiful lake on a clear Irish day. Seeing lots of sheep now, Chris said that highland sheep don't jump in front of you, but lowland sheep do.

We climbed the hills toward two megalithic mounds. The passage to the tombs was too small to enter, and it was clear to me that due to its northwestern orientation toward

Queen Maeve's tomb

Maeve's Tomb this was likely created this way for some astronomical reason.

We returned and I went up to my room, but it was too nice outdoors to take a nap, and I was too excited from Carrowkeel. I went down to the lake, along the carriage road, and kept going after the fallen tree. After about ¼ mile along the edge of the lake.

I went back to the edge of the lake, stood there for quite a while, in the elegant Yeatsean quiet, and ate my Bangor apple. The only living things visible were the birds, and the air and the lake were still, and the quiet of the countryside was tangible. I retraced my steps, back to St. Angela's. After a while the bus returned from the Sunday trip, which Mary Ann had taken, to Parke's Castle and the strand at Dun...which she said was wall-to-wall with people.

We had supper. When the subject came up (pretty standard with this bunch) that the schools are "going to the dogs" since the children are no longer required to memorize poetry, I wowed those at our table by reciting "Full many a gem..." from Gray's "Elegy."

Our entertainment after dinner was a visit from several local people who were willing to sell us their handiwork. Going to my room, I discovered I was locked out of the dorm, since we occupy using the girls' rules, but I was told how to work the combination. To bed, quite late.

July 18

Up at 7:00 AM, Monday morning, ready for breakfast and class. Martin began the class, the Story of Christianity in Ireland, playing down the role of St. Patrick, since there were Christians in Ireland before his time. I inquired about The Book of Ballymote, desiring to know if there were portions of the Brehon Law in it, but the Sligo library was, unfortunately, closed on Monday.

After dinner we walked around a little and then went to bed.

July 19

We got up at 7+/- AM, ate breakfast, and went to class, Irish History. We saw slides of the Normans and other aspects of Irish history. We heard little about the famed lengthy Protestant-Catholic "Troubles," despite my expectations.

After lunch we visited Lissadel House, the home of Constance and Eva Gore-Booth, both of whom were visited by William Butler Yeats, when he lived in Sligo. Constance, "Con," was the first female MP in Ireland. Later we saw Creevykeel, a Mesolithic court tomb excavated by a team from Harvard in the 1930s. The reconstruction, sadly, hides the true nature of this site.

Creevykeel

We got back on the bus, drove to Breencliffe, which we had passed 4 or 5 times without stopping, to look at the small church there, and Yeats' tomb, and the high cross.

It's a small church, built by Yeats' grandfather, and Yeats' marker is modest, with his own words inscribed, "...cast a cold eye on death, horsemen pass by."

William Butler Yeats was a modest man, eventually a little surprised by his success, and never totally satisfied as he wandered this vale of tears. We went the 5 or 6 miles back to St. Angela's, just in time for dinner.

After dinner we took a long walk along the lake again. Then we went to the final party at St. Angela's. The same people performed as performed at Bangor. After the farewell party we went to bed.

July 20

We got up, ate breakfast, and prepared for our departure from St. Angela's. I was sad to see the last of the nice girls in Dermot's crew.

That day we saw Knock, the site of the "visitation" around 1850. Seventeen individuals, of all ages, witnessed the apparition, perhaps it was Mary. Later we saw Galway, and then returned home.

We went to bed after a short walk.

July 21

We got up at 7:00, went upstairs for our breakfast in the common room in our dorm unit. After breakfast Mary Ann and I walked over to class. I felt that Olive, our instructor, knew the material – the megalithic – Celtic – early Christian stuff that Martin and Joyce spent their time talking about.

After class we went to lunch. We signed up for the second bunch to visit the Hunt Museum that afternoon. We walked over to the museum, which was in the basement of one of the university buildings. Terese met us, and delivered us to a museum person, who explained what they had. It was assembled by a dealer in antiquities, his personal collection, and consisted of 100+/- extremely elegant examples from all periods. The spear points were the best.

We had dinner, and then went to a cabaret entertainment at Jury's Hotel. I suppose you would call it a variety show. There were 2 male singers, 2 female, 2 Irish dancers, a stand-up comic, a violinist, a pianist, and a harpist. They were glad to see us go, making room for the regular Irish who get cranked up about that time. We went home and went to bed.

July 22

We got up 7ish, had breakfast, and went to class. Olive talked about the Celts, and gave us generally the next part of Irish history down to The Famine.

After class we had lunch at the Paddock. Our afternoon trip was to Limerick, to view the town. Afterward walked down by the river, near the abandoned warehouses being upscaled. We reloaded and rode back to Plassey village, which was the name of our dorm complex.

After dinner we were entertained in the village common room by a small group of Irish singers, players, and a dancer. Not everyone came, and it turned out to be intimate. We enjoyed the interplay with this group, and the people who came were enthusiastic. Afterwards we went home and went to bed.

July 23

We got up at 7:00, and after I shaved I went upstairs to the breakfast room where the eight of us had breakfast. At a quarter to nine we boarded the bus to tour the Burren region. We retraced our route through Limerick, pausing for a second on the street outside of Jury's Hotel to add Olive, our lecturer.

As the day went on, everyone seemed to think Olive was our best tour guide. I am not certain I have a comparative tour guide theory. While visiting an old church ruin at Killefaron Olive didn't overwhelm us with explanation of this site, which seemed to suit everyone. We took a short ride on to a tiny town with an old cathedral, part in ruins, part in use, which contains two elegant statues of bishops from the 12th century, and an old high cross immediately behind. I think this tiny village is relatively new to the joys and rigors of tourism. Later we arrived at our lunch restaurant, a new, attractive structure with a beautiful view of

Again visiting the majestic Cliffs of Moher

Galway Bay, and several miles of beach, etc.

After lunch I went down and watched some long-legged sea birds, unfamiliar to me, which were a long way off but clearly visible in my binoculars. The birds stood on a point of rocks jutting out into the water, and from time to time two of them would soar off, gliding and flying, going a mile or so into the distance, sometimes close to the water, at other times up to 50+/- feet above it. We got on the bus and drove along increasingly switch-back roads, until we reached the Cliffs of Moher.

This is one of the spectacular views of Western Europe, and on this warmest, brightest afternoon of the 1994 season, was crowded with day-trippers of all descriptions: Germans, Irish, young, old, American back-packers, etc. Below us all were careening seagulls, terns swirling around huge air currents, an active surf and a 300 ft vertical cliff. Breathtaking.

When I got almost to the bottom I saw Mary Ann, coming toward me with the news that there was a whale out there, and we hastened to the overlook, and sure enough, about ½ mile out, there was a whale, breaking the surface, showing his back, and going down for a moment or two before he came back up. Everyone seemed to have enjoyed this place.

We all shared some jokes. One – Casey went to the doctor because he was feeling bad – and the doctor said, "I can't find anything wrong with you so I suppose it must be the result of overindulgence in alcohol," and Casey said, "Oh, that's all right, doctor. I'll come back when you're sober" and on and on.

After retracing our route along the increasingly-familiar way to the university, we got home. We went over to the student union restaurant, had a very good ham supper, at a small table with the Lees. Our housing complex is increasingly occupied with youngsters going to computer camp. Then we walked across the main road to a convenience store to buy bananas and oranges for breakfast, then home, a shower, and to bed.

July 24

On this Sunday morning we arose as usual, had breakfast, and we went off for a walk along the Shannon, or the slightly smaller river which joins it near the university. We walked through the campus, later drove through Cashel, saw an abbey razed by Cromwell, and visited a well-preserved Hiberno-Gothic castle and saw the famous stone on which the descendants of Brian Boru were crowned. That evening I requested the musical act (two girls: one with a fiddle, the other with a harp) play "Brian Boru's March," which they did.

We climbed back up to the parking lot, back home, and to bed.

July 25

We got up, went upstairs to our little common room and had breakfast. Then we went over to our class, which was about Ireland from 1860-1921. Our morning lectures here were rigorous – Olive covered a lot of material. She also didn't accept questions until the end, which made for greater efficiency. She wasn't pushing any thesis, except possibly a general yearning for decency, and the slow emergence of Ireland from its chronically depressed status. After our classes, we ate lunch in the paddock.

We walked along the Shannon again that day. At some point we went to bed.

July 26

We got up, had breakfast, and walked over to class, our last. It was an interesting class. Olive was talking about the things that she thought about every day, to an audience that was receptive, but did not have her perspective at all. She is intelligent, and was enjoying the chance to explain her point of view, that Ireland should move ahead keeping the most valuable ways of the past, making a better life for everyone, to the extent possible. She was also learning from us, adjusting her point of view a very small amount, on the basis of questions and discussion. She tried to explain the difference between Sinn Fein and the IRA and explain the talks that were being shown on the morning news.

At one point, Olive said that the strategy was to get the extremists to talk, so that everyone could learn the poverty of their ideas. At the end I threw out the point that in Eastern Europe there are now many countries with problems similar to those in Ireland. Ireland is much less devastating than in Yugoslavia, or Lithuania, and that possibly the techniques and procedures that are being developed could become a model to help others. My fellow EHers took this in with totally blank looks (a standard response to a non-standard idea).

Another major line though was tracing the evolution of the Common-EEC-ED-EU (European Union) and Ireland's participation. Ireland feels different to me than it did five years ago, probably because of its EC ties – there are lots of new dwellings, and a slightly more prosperous look.

At any rate, our last class was well-received, and though many in the group were tired of classes, Olive finished on an up beat, we gave her a round of applause, and off to the Paddock for lunch. We ate and walked back.

In the afternoon we took a trip to Bunratty Castle and the attached folk village. Our tour guide was Therese. As we went through Old Limerick we saw a circular sign (historical marker), which said, "MacNamara's Band." I later asked Therese but she didn't know the sign was there. We went over the now-familiar streets of Limerick, past Jury's Hotel, on the road that leads to Shannon Airport. The castle at Bunratty is about 20 minutes from the university, and 5 miles from the airport.

Bunratty Castle, Limerick

I climbed up the spiral stairs to the turret, where you could see the River Shannon not too far away, and the small stream that went right by the castle.

The dinners in Limerick were good – not large portions, but that was fine with me. We went to the common room for our final party together. We were given a glass of wine as we entered. The party started off with a poetry reading, not too well scheduled. The lady read Yeats, mainly poems that had been better presented in Sligo. Then each of us was supposed to recite a limerick, or otherwise perform. Mary Ann's limerick was:

> "There once was a group on a bus/Who traveled without any fuss/They loved to shop/At every stop/And hopped back on when they must."

And mine:

> "There once was a young man from Sligo/Who aspired to play at Iago/TV ratings did soar/We're all waiting for more/As O.J. excels as Othello."

The total number who performed was about ½ of those assembled. The final act was our 83-year-old guitarist August, with the Willie Nelson style of delivery. All but about 15 slipped out the door before he got set up. Mary Ann grabbed me just as I was about to slip away, and said it wouldn't be right. After his first song most of us abandoned him. We went to our unit, and turned in.

July 27

We got up and went up to our Spartan breakfast.

We got on the bus, about 2/3 of the group, for the short ride to Shannon to catch the 9:00 AM flight to Heathrow. We went to the duty free shop. It just opened up as we sat there. It was my impression that the duty free shop in Shannon has a bigger selection and better prices than those other places. As we prepared to board there was one uniformed policeman and three men in business suits carefully examining those about to board. There had been bombings in the preceding days, and a car bomb headed for the Channel had been intercepted about the time we arrived three weeks ago. Our passports were not checked, either here or at Heathrow later in the morning.

There was a very long walk to our baggage, partly on moving sidewalks. We transferred it to the red bus headed toward the Marriott, under our tour guide Katherine's watchful eye, and at about 10:00 made our way to the center of London. The train workers in England had been striking on Wednesdays most of the summer, and while our plan was to take the Underground, it was not clear how this would be affected by the strike. We bought day passes for the Underground and bus system, for 3 pounds 70 pence each, and joined forces with Amy Lee for our tour. Her husband Clarence preferred to go to the Marriott, and she was not uncomfortable with the thought of going by herself, but seemed satisfied to join us.

Our next target was the National Gallery, across the street from Trafalgar Square. The ride in was about 50 minutes, with one transfer at Green Park, then to Westminster. Amy had a conversation on the train with a young Indian girl, about 25 I suppose, who told her she was a doctor and had been practicing for three years. We came up from underground into a hot sunshiny day, the square mobbed with tourists mainly. But the square is surrounded by large buildings, the

National Gallery, London

National Gallery on one whole side, and an infinite number of traffic buses, taxis and trucks mostly.

We worked our way up to the entrance to the gallery, which had a large sign that read, "Free today and every day." I wanted to see their Picassos (to see what they had, and what they thought of it), and we picked up a very nice one-page floor plan that directed us to the East Wing. The East Wing was right there, up a flight of stairs, and to the right. Picasso was the last painter exhibited, and they had some definitive 1912 cubist paintings (perhaps 2 or 3), and in the other room two very nice Dora Maar's by Picasso and 5 or 6 other paintings and a statue, all from a collection. The display took a large jump backward, to Ce'zanne, with several paintings, a portrait and some landscapes. There was a large Seurat, a major work, and three or four striking Van Gogh's. One of my favorites was a Monet of the little garden bridge at Giverny, which was stereopticon at 40 feet. There was an elegant Houses of Parliament, brighter than most of the ones in the exhibit here, delicate and fine. There was a room of Turners, including one huge one of a ship in a stormy sea that had glass over it. I asked the guard if he knew why it was behind glass, and he told me that it was a condition of the anonymous lender. There were some monumental Constables, the Reynolds of Tarleton and Mrs. Siddons, etc.

We changed wings to look at Rembrants. There was one room with monumental portraits, including a Rembrandt of William of Orange on a horse, which dominated the scene. There was another room containing Rembrandts exclusively: a Saskia in the stream, two self portraits, and others. Next door there was a room full of students of Rembrandt, and a pair of pictures, one by a student, which was formerly attributed to Rembrandt, and a terse explanation that Rembrandt couldn't have done that. I suppose I believed it – the details were done by different hands.

House of Parliament, London

By *this* time we were beginning to flag, and I suggested that we make for the Brasserie for something, which turned out to be a baguette for me, which was brie, and a croissant with butter and jam for Mary Ann, and tea. Places to eat in galleries are nice, perhaps the people who work there are genteel and the casuals are ethereal. At any rate, we agreed we should abandon the gallery, and go down to Westminster Abbey and the Houses of Parliament. There was a short walk and we were in the free zone, looking at graves of lesser men, Dr. Livingston (or so I presumed), Robert Louis Stephenson...and up to the gate (3 pounds) to greater glories. There was a mob, some being lectured, some not, and it was difficult to imagine what it was like for a royal wedding.

Then we went out and wandered along Parliament, and out onto the bridge a few feet to get a better view. This is one of the world's greatest buildings, and on a hot summer afternoon, in the middle of a sweltering mob and barely moving congested traffic, it sits like a Buddha over it all. All three of us wanted to sit down, so we made our way to St. James Park. We got on The Underground, squeezing in to a very hot, jam-packed car.

A man in the immediate vicinity was dripping wet. I asked a man jammed up against me if the crowding was a result of the strike and he said yes; that he, for example, would have been on a train, except for the strike.

We rode for thirty minutes or so, and transferred to another section when the blue line split. The transfer took 3 or 4 minutes, and finally we were delivered up to Heathrow 123, not knowing quite where to go to catch the red Marriott shuttle. We muddled around, and caught a bus as it was leaving, being the only passengers at 5:00. Who knew where the luggage was? It turned out it was all in our room. We bathed, then went down to the bar and had two expensive glasses of white wine (one each). I found a seat by two old guys who had been in Scotland learning about whiskey, and they wanted to know where I'd been, and did I have a good time. I said, "Oh yes." Then we went in to dinner. After dinner we took a brief stroll out on the grounds, walked one loop of the jogging trail, and off to bed.

July 28

We got up at 6:00 AM, so our luggage could be picked up at 8:00 for delivery at Heathrow two hours in advance. All of the EHers had breakfast in the banquet room. It was not nearly so nice as our arrival breakfast, but we ate with Catherine our tour leader, and others. Catherine wanted to talk about herself. She was off to visit a friend somewhere in the country, and didn't have another group for a month or so. She doesn't like all of the evaluation, and it is not a trivial responsibility keeping 37 geriatrics happy, and mobile.

After breakfast we hung around for a while waiting to leave, left into a serious traffic jam which put us a little late into Heathrow. But, after being thoroughly grilled by an Indian security guard, we checked our bags and got our boarding passes. On the flight I dozed a while and soon we were over Newfoundland. It is not easy to tell where you are at 17,000 feet, where the waters and land below are equal in extent, with little or no indication of human occupation.

We were dropped off, called a taxi, and delivered home at 11:30 PM+/-. This is THE END of our trip to Wales and Ireland this summer.

EASTERN CANADA

My mother's family immigrated to Canada from New York. They landed in St. John in 1778 and immediately went up the river, narrowly escaping the cholera epidemic that killed half of those who remained in St. John. The Loyalist heritage, of which my family was a part, has been a large factor in the direction of Canadian history.

The descendents of early French settlers of Canada have not been absorbed into the larger culture, and remain a force, cohesive but not very happy.

Ninety percent of the Canadian population lives within 100 miles of the border with the United States.

August 6, 1995

THIS IS THE JOURNAL OF OUR TRIP TO CANADA THIS SUMMER: NOVA SCOTIA AND NEW BRUNSWICK

The ride to Atlanta was shockingly uneventful.

When we got to the airport it was only 30 feet from the van to the check-in. The Sunday morning bunch going to Canada is different from our fellow travelers to England a year ago: younger, more diverse. As our plane was about to be announced a group of 15+/- young oriental girls sat down across the way, and we saw two or three T-shirts with team China on them; I guessed it was the volleyball team, on the basis of their size and shape. The older woman in charge came over and greeted two hawk-faced occidental women in the next row of seats, and they became animated, and then she went across to her girls and came back with one, and said, "She understands English." Unfortunately, this is all I heard.

Our flight was all above the clouds, and bright and sunny. We got a very nice view of the Toronto skyline, with the World's Fair Needle in the near distance as we gained altitude to the cruising level. The cloud cover obscured everything, until just before the coast, of Maine, I suppose. Across the Bay of Fundy we got good views, both fore and aft, of the two coastlines. Nova Scotia does not seem very populated from up there — Not many dwellings visible, or roads, just a lot of lakes and rivers, and second growth forests.

As we approached Halifax the view of the harbor was good, and we could see the high bridge and extensive layout of the harbor, according to the air line magazine blurb, the second largest natural harbor in the world.

Bay of Fundy, Nova Scotia

We engaged a taxi to take us to Wolfeville, for $89 Canadian. The young man was garrulous, and (when asked) told us he had been born on Prince Edward Island, worked in southern Alberta for the power company, and in Toronto for a while, but had been in Halifax for 12 years. He went to Florida one winter, but except for the sunshine, didn't enjoy it much because there wasn't anything to do. Around Halifax everything was second growth pines and hardwood, with lots of little lakes, and rocks.

Finally, after half an hour, as we approached the Bay of Fundy, we came into the rolling meadows of the Avon valley, dairy farms and orchards. We had several elegant panoramas, of the river, the Bay and the green fields stretching to the purple hills on the horizon. The farms and houses are all very well-kept, with very few ramshackle structures. We finally arrived at Wolfeville, a town of 3000, a support town for Acadia University, with bookstores, pizza places, photographers with graduation pictures in their displays, small arty enterprises. We had missed the beginning meeting and meal at our Elderhostel. I hope this hasn't blotted our copybook indelibly, but we will find out. So, after we had been given our room key we walked the quarter mile to town and had supper. After supper we walked another quarter mile to the parking lot, where there was a nice view across a tidal inlet, and the tide was more or less out. This is a green meadowland as far as you can see off toward the bay.

August 7

The next morning we got up early, partly from excitement, partly from anxiety about the adequacy of the bathroom facilities in our dorm. We had breakfast. Then we had class. The first hour was taught by a woman named Heather, who was representing a company which had, at great expense ($100,000), prepared by a satellite photograph of the Maritimes. It is a beautiful photograph.

During the second hour, we heard a long lecture by Sherman Williams, our main lecturer, painting us a lovely picture of the tides. He covered much of the material in the article he handed out. He's a good lecturer, and he had thought about every aspect of the natural history of the Bay of Fundy. He is an enthusiastic lecturer and enjoys talking to us, and has heard every question many times. He gave us a theory that the exceptional high tides in the Bay of Fundy are due in part to a reasonable phenomenon. We had a long video of the tides at Cape Split, the most extreme flow of ocean water anywhere, and it was impressive. He has supplied us with numerous maps and graphs, with all kinds of tide data for today, and the rest of our visit. He has a very nice sine wave graph for the tides, with the graph for the much lower tides of Halifax superimposed.

In the evening we went to a variety show at the theater, put on as a fundraiser for the theater season, of which this is the first. I saw a variety show in the church near grandfather's farm when I was a boy, and I tried to convince Mary Ann that this was a continuation of a tradition from colonial times, but she was skeptical. The skits were a stand-up comic, the stage hands singing a comedy song, the impresario reading a (comic) letter, the younger leads with sonnets by Shakespeare and Edna St. Vincent Mallay in a sketch about love, and a couple of 50s type songs by the resident actors. It was fun, but we quit at the half. They were to conduct an auction, in which we had no intention of bidding.

Behind the dormitory when we got back, Sherman had set up two telescopes...a small refractor and a 10-inch Dobsonian, so we could look at the moon, and the moons of Jupiter, which were nicely lined up. There was a lot of light pollution, but it didn't interfere with the project, which was Sherman giving the interested persons in his class the rudiments of star watching. We were in the crowd of 15 or so and stayed for 20 minutes, taking short turns at the scopes.

August 8

We got up, 6:30ish, and went to breakfast. Then we had a briefing about our field trip for the day, which included a shore drive along the shore of the Minas Basin, a pause on the Wellington Dyke, and finally, a walk out into the marsh. These things all happened, and were interesting. We could see sea gulls from the dyke, and among them some sandpipers. At high tide, they don't feed, but sit relatively quietly, since their food is well under water.

Then we looked at a wharf that had fallen into disrepair (Delhaven). At one point (75 years ago) it was a ferry stop, and the primary mode of transportation for the area. Then we had lunch in Blomidon Park, a relatively new provincial park, and our picnic area had 6 or 8 tables in a big green meadow. Our lunch was croissant sandwiches. There was a great view out into the Basin, glimpses of which we could catch through the pines. Mary Ann and I, bad citizens, grabbed good seats at the table, while the less Elderhsotlers had to sit on the grass or stand.

Then, after lunch, we had a leisurely stroll through a portion of the park, where we could look out at various places, and see the distant islands, and the various color changes on the surface as the tide came in. More or less, near our lookouts, the water was a little choppy, then when I first started looking, there was a line of demarcation about ⅓ of the way across, on the other side, which was quite a bit calmer. Then, as we watched, the line receded toward the far shore. It was a beautiful sunny day, and the sun and breeze also contributed to what we were seeing. As we went along Sherman lectured us about botany. We saw a little hedgehog on the road, who skittered off into the woods as 4 or 5 Elderhostlers surged to get a look. Mary Ann saw him vanish over a little ridge in the trees. While we pursued this distraction we missed some important point in Sherman's explanation, but I didn't know what it was.

There were six or eight campsites through the trees as we walked along. This may have been one of the best weeks of the summer for campers here.

Next up for we intrepid Eldershostlers was a biology experiment. We were provided with plastic trays with which to collect and study these things. The ground underfoot varied from dry to covered with water. Sherman carefully explained which grasses needed almost all day dry, to those that could stand most of it underwater. Then, after a while, we got on the bus and made our way back to our dormitory, a somewhat tired and bedraggled elderly group. It was interesting to see our fellow boarders, the high school girls' basketball camp looking equally punched out after their day on the courts, or wherever they were.

We were given a barbecue for dinner, and it was a pleasant meal in the banquet room for us – barbecued chicken, very good potato salad, other salad,...and strawberry shortcake.

After dinner we went to hear a lecture about Alex Colville, who is an important 20th century painter who lives in Wolfeville. He was an official artist for the Canadian military in WWII. He painted the worst things that happened, including one of the German extermination camps. Then, when he came back he taught for a few years (2 or 3) and then launched out on his own. It was 10 years or so before his work was recognized. His pictures are almost exclusively autobiographical. The pictures have always some non-trivial menace or tension. But the Canadians love him. He even designed their coins. The movie had comments by him, which counteracts one of my theories, that painters do not consciously have elaborate intentions, at several levels. They make a good picture, and then other people supply the motivation. But I liked the pictures I saw, but not better than Picasso.

The girl who lectured afterwards in the display of seriographs was a true acolyte. She talked for 20 minutes without stopping, and seemed prepared to keep going. I finally decided I had to look at the prints. There was one of a man with his hands on a cow that was good — And a nice view of the bay outside Wolfeville, etc.

It is all interesting.

Home and to bed.

August 9

The next morning we left for an all-day field trip, this time lots of views from the top of the North mountain, which is a substantial wind break for the Annapolis Valley. The preparatory talk was in a geology lab, and we were shown numerous rocks, and to be taken to a beach where you could pick them up, at Hall's Harbor.

Minas Basin

Before that we had several views of Cape Split and the Minas Basin, and we walked around at the look-off and the harbor, where it was substantially cooler, and then went up for lunch at the farm of the route guide, our agricultural expert, who is also the father-in-law of our tour coordinator, Judy, whose husband grows apples and gladiolas commercially. Her father-in-law, Fred Walsh, led us through his extensive garden, in which he has planted a tree for the numerous events of his life, and he has them all marked. The births of his children, his quarrels with his wife,...can be traced in his garden tour. I don't believe I could do this — There are too many nuances. Actually he said he knew that Di and Charles were in trouble when their wedding tree lost a big limb which almost hit the house. He showed us his huge orchard, apples, and some of the many techniques he had invoked to increase the yield. I couldn't understand much of it — he planted a row immediately adjacent, a foot away, from every row, and they were all staked, and a perforated plastic tube sunk down by the roots, but I am not certain why.

His wife invited Mary Ann and me to have lunch in her kitchen, which was a very kind thing. It was a little bit like *The Bridges of Madison County* — The scene with the family eating before embarking for the fair. Mrs. Walsh was there, keeping track of everything which was going on. I suppose we are a little too house-proud to be able to let strangers wander around as they were. Then we got on the bus and drove by a huge mound of sand that his son had piled up, to be sold at some point in the future when the price is right.

Then we went to see a commercial cranberry bog. It is the largest in Nova Scotia. There are 6 or 8 banked areas, which can be flooded if necessary, and the mechanical pickers float and comb the plants. The man who manages the farm talked to us, but he wasn't sure that was what he wanted to be doing. We walked around for 20 minutes or so, then piled back on the bus. We finally went home by the eagle's nest...no eagles at the moment, unfortunately.

After dinner, we relaxed and went to bed.

August 10

It is a pity that I have waited so long to get this down, because this was a truly elegant day for us, and I am sure that many of the details have slipped away. We got up at 6:30 AM and it was a sunny morning, dew on the grass as we walked across the campus, 5 minute walk, to Wheelock Hall, where all of our meals were served. The meals catered by Marriott, and were very good, we had fresh oranges and grapefruit, and eggs on French toast or pancakes. The toast machine was very slow, and getting coffee and water was tricky, but once you got the formula, it was fine. There was usually a mob of girl basketball campers, or dance camp or somebody, sharing the line with us, and this was very pleasant for us. We were scheduled to go see the tidal bore at Sussex. The preparatory talk was in our main room and dealt with the bore, but after a little while we got on the bus and headed out. Sherman had exactly figured out when we should be at the tidal bore farm, and so we visited a gypsum grinding mill and saw, as we rode along, quite a few gypsum outcrops, and a town or two, and just about 10:30 we crossed a key bridge and climbed the hill to the Tidal Bore View Farm. Sherman was thinking about something else, and we slipped past the entrance and had to go back.

Tidal Bore View Farm

The Tidal Bore View Farm was not very well-kept, and the owner had discovered what he liked to do, namely, tell people about the tidal bore. We were invited to contribute (but not required – I put it $2) and he had constructed a rail and a few seats along a ridge overlooking a 20+/- acre mud flat, where we were told, the bore would soon appear. The setting was superb – and right on the dot, a two foot wall of water came down the distant river, going 6+/- miles an hour. When it got to the mud flat, it separated, and the two waves circled around the mud flat, and met below out viewing spot, and quickly began the process of inundating the surrounding area. The circling process took 5+/- minutes, and it was probably 15 minutes before the whole 20 acres was under water. Before this happened, we all hopped on the bus, and raced down the hill, to see it appear again, watching from the bridge. It was probably ½ mile down the road. There were perhaps 20 people already at the bridge, and with our 41, there was a little mob scene. About 2 minutes after we got out of the bus and onto the bridge, the bore came into sight again, coming toward us at 6 mph. In some ways it was like a breaker on one of our Southern beaches, but the surge of the front, with the force of the low wall of water behind gives a feeling of relentlessness.

Tidal Bore View Farm

We hurried along the side of the road — The river makes an S curve there. We managed to see it again. The low hills, marsh grass near the edge, and the beauty of the spot, make this one of Nature's 7 Wonders.

We jumped back on the bus and to the better seats than yesterday, when we landed on top of the rear wheels. I figured we should take our turn over the wheels, but that it wasn't a life sentence. So I scrambled for a better seat this day, when we started out. We drove a few miles to a provincial park to look at the birds. We climbed up on the bank of the Avon River, and there were lots of gulls and sandpipers across the way, and a heron, about ¼ mile over on the mud flat. This mud flat was very active, at the crustacean level, since a causeway had been recently built for the road, I suppose, creating a fresh water lake on the other side. We climbed back on the bus and got back to lunch about 12:00.

The lunches, as always, were good dorm fare. After lunch we walked back to our room, across the green campus. By this time we had the most efficient route figured out, and didn't go out of our way seeing new parts of the campus and surrounding area. The area adjoining the campus was all supporting, professors' houses, apartments for younger faculty and students, one or two that looked like rooming houses. Once, when we were walking by one of these we heard an agonizing shout, perhaps a disturbed person, and I told Mary Ann I'd think twice before I rented a room there. But everything here is remarkably well-kept — The people are house-proud, and the campus merges into the surrounding area and almost without a boundary. Everyone has nice flowers, in bloom now.

I decided to go to the Alumni House, which is on the main street of Wolfeville, across the street from University Hall, to see if I could find traces of mother. I walked into the very nice Victorian house and looked around the two or three downstairs rooms, which were elegantly furnished with turn of the century antiques. There was no one in sight, so I hesitantly climbed the stairs, and at the end of the hall there was a reception desk, and a receptionist on duty. She was well-chosen for her position — A blonde, attractive, confident, 35+/- yr. old Acadian, who, when I explained my mission, called up mother's name on her computer immediately. I was very pleased that I had mother's graduation year right, and all of my remembered data agreed with theirs.

Mother graduated in 1913, and got a Master's Degree in 1914. They had mother's last address in Italy, but not the fact that she died there. So I went downstairs and added that to the data bank, my contact there being another (obvious) Acadian lady with a more computer-familiar look. I volunteered myself as mother's next of kin in the database. The receptionist had directed me to the archives in the library, after looking to see if they had a yearbook in 1913, which they did not.

Acadia College graduating class of 1914

So, I walked across the street to the main library, and was directed by the circulation desk to the basement where the archives and the QAs (math books) were. I was met by a student assistant. The lady across the street had phoned ahead, and the young man was quickly able to produce a photograph of mother's graduation class, and some copies of the literary magazine, the "Acadia Athenaeun," in which I found two elegant photographs, one of which was mother as a member of the basketball team, the other the cast of a play in which she had a part. There were several other references which I did not write down or copy. But I did copy one which says:

"Basketball. After the football game there was a basketball game in the gymnasium between the college girls of Mt. Allison and Acadia which resulted in a victory for the latter with a score of 17-14. The game was most exciting and very closely contested. The first half ended with the score 6-6. Both teams played well, the playing of Miss Cash of Mt. A. and Miss Van Wart of Acadia being especially worthy of mention.

I was very excited. The young man very nicely made some copies for me, but I decided not to take very much. One of the things that I did not take was the class prophesy for mother, in which it was predicted, "...that she would go West, and be very religious."

Both of these things did happen, and as soon as I saw the prophesy I knew I did not want to study it, because mother was the kind of person who might have been influenced by a class prophecy, and say, refused a proposal on the basis that the prophecy would be contradicted, and that my existence hinged on the idle musing of a dumb Acadian. Best not to think about it.

I had to rush out to get under closing time, quickly speed read the

QAs, which dealt mainly with computing (the main QAs are in the science library), and stuff like that. Mary Ann had joined me at this point.

After supper, several of us got in a van, and Sherman took us to see the low tide and sunset at Hall Harbor, which was 15+/- miles away. We drove through the countryside, now becoming familiar, and finally reached the harbor, where the formerly floating boats were resting in the mud alongside the wharf. I bought a large bag of dulse in a weather-beaten store. There were several people in the store, and I had to be pushy tourist because Sherman had plans for us.

We walked across a little bridge over the little stream which fed into the harbor, up a slight hill onto the wharf. On the wharf they were boiling and serving lobsters, and 3 or 4 picnic tables were being used by tourists, the ones I saw mainly young people on dates, having a good time. The man selling lobsters held up a 5-pounder ($35) for our inspection. We walked out to the end of the wharf, and the sun, across the bay, had about ½ hour to go until sunset. So we walked back across the bridge, and up the hill, to the house of an elderly lady, who was one of Sherman's first colleagues when he started teaching. The house was a summer cottage, and while it was smaller, it had the feeling of the cottage we rented at Mispec. Same kind of windows, furnished the same way, a nice porch looking out into the bay. There were two other ladies visiting, and Sherman introduced us around, and we talked about Elderhostel, and other non-controversial subjects, and then went outside, and I looked at a tree that had fallen over the cliff while Sherman worried that I was going to slip over the edge. Since he was my host I figured he could make the rules, so I came back from the edge. By this time the sun was very near to setting, and we all watched the last few minutes hoping for the green flash. We didn't see one. Mary Ann was being sweet with our fellow Elderhostlers.

We walked back down the hill, got in the van, and retraced our route back to our dorm at Acadia. It had been an extremely memorable day for me: the tidal bore, finding mother's picture, and sunset over the Bay of Fundy. **A person who has such things has enough**.

August 11

We got up, ate breakfast and walked to our class in the Beveridge Art Center.

That morning Sherman brought a whale vertebra and a stuffed bald eagle. Fred talked first, more or less a summary of his talks, and he answered questions, which seemed to me to be asked for politeness, at least some of them. Then we had our break and I had a half glass of lemonade, as usual. Then Sherman did his recap, talking about his subjects. He asked a question, "Why does the time of high tide advance day after day?" I was able to answer nicely – "Because the lunar and solar calendars do not coincide." This impressed several Elderhostlers. Sherman elaborated, graciously saying, "That's it in a nutshell."

Then we went to lunch. After lunch Sherman had offered to take those interested on a birding hike. There weren't too many of us, and we all fit into his van. We made our way through the land behind the dikes near Grand Pre' to a spot on the dike where we could look out across the Minas Basin. There were birds to be seen – gulls and black-billed plovers, and others, but Sherman thought we would have better luck at a point further along. So we piled back in the van, and drove a mile or so, through the fields, to the house of a friend of his from his ornithology club. She had placed chairs out on the mud flat. So we sat and watched an extremely nice ornithological sight — which had been explained to us by Sherman earlier.

At high tide the mud flats are covered, and the primary source of food for the sandpipers is not available to them. So they sit just at the high tide line, almost immobile, some times among the flock of gulls, who also don't move around much then. Five or ten minutes later, after high tide, as the mud flat uncovers, they are out very vigorously feeding on the small crustaceans. The other thing that happens, in August, at high tide, is that they collect in large flocks, several thousand birds, and swoop around the Basin. This is a spectacular display since they flash dark and white as they change directions in their soaring. It is conjectured that this flocking and soaring is aimed at discouraging predators, the falcons and the hawks that like sandpipers for lunch. As we watched we could see large flocks merge and separate, for who knows what reason.

I sat on the bank in a chair, next to William, I think, and he agreed when I said I thought this was a birding "hot spot," a technical term I have learned from reading Bird Watcher's Digest. He also agreed when I said that I know people who would travel a thousand miles to watch it. We were there perhaps a half an hour or more — Sherman went down the cliff to the flat to get photographs. But thought it was too risky for us to do that. Then he suggested we move over to the adjoining property, where the view of the sandpipers beginning to work on the mudflat was better.

While looking at this bunch I spotted two or three stilt sandpipers and pointed them out to Ramsey Ross, from Moose Jaw, who seemed to be a birder, but who was reluctant to hazard a guess as to what it was. Maybe he wants his list to contain super confirmed species or something. But we were passing around Peterson's (mine and Sherman's). Ramsey seemed younger than the average person in our group, younger than 60 years old anyway, but except for a short conversation early on, when I learned that he worked for the government in Moose Jaw, I didn't talk to him. After 10 minutes or so we ambled back to the van, looking at the barn and house on this property, and went back to get ready for our final banquet. We were deposited at our dorm, rested a few minutes, then walked over to Wheelock, to the Lounge, and the seafood banquet.

The Lounge was set up very nicely, with a cash bar for the Happy (half) Hour that seems to be part of Elderhostel closings. I had water, and Mary Ann a glass of white wine, I think, before we went in to the buffet. I was not very circulatory, since I was preparing in my mind my contribution to the entertainment. The buffet had been set up in a separate room, and was indeed elegant.

Fred Walsh sat with us and regaled us with his stories. One of them involved the celebration/riot which occurred in Halifax on V.E. Day in 1945. He was very young at the time, 10+/-, and his father was going on. When they got there, it was a true celebration – sailors had looted the liquor stores, and there was public lovemaking, and his father drove him away as fast as he could. I told him that I had participated in such a celebration, on VJ Day, when the Japanese capitulated. I was on a shipping list to go to prepare for the invasion of Japan, and in three days my life was totally turned around.

I had spoken earlier to his daughter-in-law, Judy Walsh, who was our coordinator, and told her that I was prepared to read some of mother's poems, and she decided to schedule me first. In the event there were two other poets (Sherman and someone thanking our Elderhostel lecturers and support, I think).

I felt good about my reading. I introduced it by saying that mother had graduated from Acadia in 1913, and then read, "To an island near my old home," "St. John, "In dock," and the prose paragraphs about the St. John River in the obituary for Eva Snow. Those are Maritime Province-inspired. Then I read four about nature: "That Red Bird," "Yellow," "Cherry Trees," and "Summer Midnight."

My presentation wasn't quite as good as I would have liked. My original plan was to speak without the microphone, which I have almost never used, and adjust my vocal force to the right level as I read. But as I started, some stupid Elderhostel person in the back yelled, "Use the Mic!" so I did, and transferred my poems to my left hand which is subject to inherited tremors. But the reading went well, and I received applause after each poem.

The next item on the schedule was a slide presentation by Gene Garret, from Huntsville, Alabama, of photographs he had taken during an Elderhostel stay in southern Mexico. He had integrated some Mexican music into his presentation, and made various comments about his photographs as he went through the sequence. This presentation was a big thing to him (just as mine was to me). I was still flying high on the adrenaline from my little effort, and couldn't concentrate much on his, which lasted for 20 minutes. Mary Ann said his pictures were beautiful, and told him so, but I felt they weren't that much better than the ones she takes.

Next, the man who was greens keeper for the golf courses at Yale, Henry Meusel, got up and told a rambling golf course joke — He went to the nearby golf course, and walked out on the #1 fairway, and said, "Oh, you have a little crab grass over there, and a little later, some...disease there"...and the guy he was with, someone from the Club, offered him a job. Just a terrible joke.

Then, in a very deep and strong bass voice he sang, "Ol' Man River" and a song in Japanese, to the youngest member of our group, the new wife of Dana Whittaker, whose name is Nikki. I enjoyed this.

Then Sherman read his poem, which wasn't a literary effort, and Judy spoke a little, and we all went back to the dorm to get ready for tomorrow's departure.

Sherman had announced a contest, the rolling of the marble-shaped stones we picked up on the beach of Hall's Harbor. Dana won the contest, and the prize was a very nice rock with a vein of amethyst in it.

August 12

We got up at 6:30 AM and walked down to the public parking to look at the mud flat there for the last time. In the 5 days the low tide has progressed 5 hours, so the mud flat was wetter than it was the first morning when we came. There was an old bicycle half-buried in the mud off the wharf, and a few gulls around. It was beautiful weather every day we were in Wolfeville, although some thought it was too hot. They have little need and no provision for air conditioning. But I think some people have less tolerance for temperature variation than I do. My biggest dislike is a draft on my back, and I always take a sweater if I think there may be one.

We walked back, myself a little sad, across to the lovely green campus, in some sense in mother's footsteps, past the small triangular rose patch, with fading flowers, which had perfumed our trips to and from meals all week.

Mary Ann had made contact with an Elderhostler in the laundry room downstairs, who was going exactly our way, and they had a van and would be willing to take us. They were Elizabeth and Carroll Hayes who live in upper New York State, above Seneca Lake. We met them after breakfast and put our bags in the van. Before that we said goodbye to several people, including Judy Walsh, our coordinator, who had brought her 7-month-old son Alexander, for us all to admire. There were 6 or 8 Elderhostlers in the vestibule, all of them googling with the baby, who was good-natured, but not absolutely certain about it all. Mary Ann tried to lay $5 on the college girl at the desk, but she couldn't take it.

Then we started out in the van toward Digby, where we were to catch the ferry to St. John. As we rode along we learned the nuts and bolts of their lives, he contracts to do solar heating, and they have three children who are spread around, none close to them, I think. He is slightly older than I am. For practical purposes we didn't talk all that much, although we were all able to comment on the geological features of the surrounding countryside much more knowledgeably than before our classes. We drove parallel to the North Mountain until we approached Yarmouth, which we did not enter, and off to Digby. It was first farms, then forests, with an occasional glimpse of a lake. When we flew in, it seemed as if there was more area in lakes than in trees, but it did not seem that way as we drove along. As we approached Digby, the Annapolis Basin opened before us, with its purple hills on the far side, and lots of dark blue water in several directions. I could see the Digby Cut, which looked quite narrow as we approached from the north. (The maps call it the Digby Neck, but I prefer the name from my youth, when we climbed to the top of the bank at Mispec, and could see it across the Bay on an especially clear day, of which there were not many.)

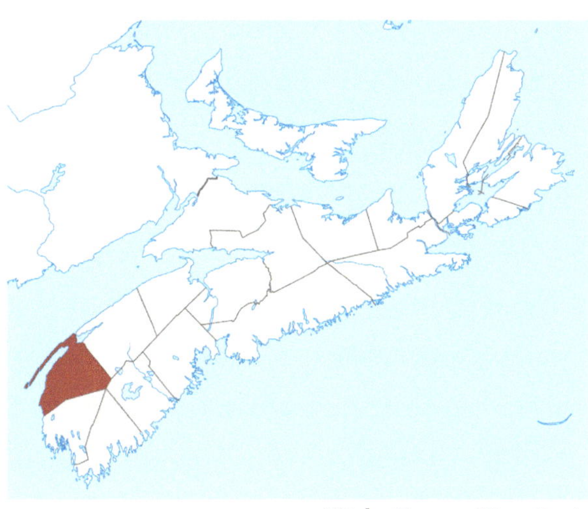

Digby County, Nova Scotia

We followed the road signs to the ferry, parked at the van, and then hurried in to the ticket office to get passage. Our tickets were $16 apiece, and I don't know what Carroll had to pay for the van. We had about 1½ hour before sailing, so we drove in to the flesh pots of Digby where they were having a scallop festival – complete with mussel shucking contest, Scotch dancing, etc. The main street of the little town was bustling. As Mary Ann and Elizabeth checked out the souvenir shops, Carroll and I walked around, and he told me some details from his early life. His father was a professor at Columbia, a history professor, specializing in modern Europe. During World War II his father was ambassador to Spain. His family flew to Spain in a Clipper Ship, the flying boat, and were the only passengers. Their last land contact was in the Bahamas, and when they took off there was a hurricane approaching, so they had to get out of there.

They lived in the house of the Duke of Alba in Madrid. It had priceless paintings, an expansive garden, big staircases and everything. He said that he was a courier, and flew to Portugal to pick up the embassy payroll. Another courier, who had gone to Switzerland to get the diplomatic pouch, which was locked to his wrist, was captured crossing occupied France, and the Nazis cut off his arm. His father had a plane assigned, to visit the consulates, and Carroll went up with the pilot, who taught him to fly. They located several places from which the Germans were jamming U.S. news broadcasts, by locating the beam of the jammer, following the beam until they were directly overhead, where the signal stopped. The jammer was in a barn or some place like that. So then they would tell the police, who would raid the location. But the jammers would be back in a week or so, operating from a new hide out.

I asked if he had been to the Alhambra in Grenada. He said he had to stay in Madrid and study mathematics when his family went there. He told me he had entered several monasteries in this country, as a novice, but then learned that that was not what he wanted to do. They were just like college faculties, with all of the tensions and pettiness of academia. I asked if he had been to Monserrat, and he said that visiting there was what made him want to become a brother. I told him about our visit when we heard the boy choir, and joined the long line of pilgrims to touch the Black Virgin.

He told me that when he was staying at Monserrat, as a lay person meditating I suppose, he went out climbing on the rocks above the monastery, and quite a ways away he stumbled onto a cave, and went in, and there were signs of use. So he followed it back, making a sharp turn, and he came out into a garden. Shortly, two monks came up, and asked how he had gotten there. It seems he had stumbled on their secret escape route, which during World War II was still a necessity. At some point a large number of monks had been liquidated, but I am not sure when that was.

Another of his stories involved his father, when he first arrived at the U.S. Embassy in Madrid. When he went to set up his office as ambassador, he was met by the resident secretary, a person who had been highly recommended in Washington, and she told the ambassador that it was the custom in this embassy that the ambassador had the outer office, and the resident secretary the inner office. The new ambassador told her that that may have been the way it was, but not anymore. He installed himself in the inner office, and in a short while discovered that it was possible to hear what was going on in the room above, through the chimney, and the room above was the code room. The woman was a spy for the Germans, and was immediately fired.

While we walked down on the dock of the little marina he told me how he had learned to sail, while he was living in a monastery in New Jersey. He had a free day each week, and went to a nearby lake and took lessons.

We rejoined the ladies, and they had started on their gift lists, and it seemed to me, mainly T-shirts.

We headed through the Cut, out into the bay. I had my small bird watching glasses, and was able to examine the shore installations, the hotel in which I had dinner in 1935,...Soon we were out in the bay, and I misidentified a cloud bank as New Brunswick. We had been told that this was very good whale watching water, but all I came up with was some pelagic birds, new to me (greater shearwaters, almost certainly). They are good-sized black birds with a slim look, and they soar and swoop and rest on the water, and are beautiful. I saw 20 or 30 of them I suppose. As we crossed, the fog got thicker toward St. John. It was breezy and cold watching for whales, and we quickly moved to the side of the ship, slightly, but not completely, protected.

We slipped into East St. John, went down into the depths to get into the van, and drove straight to the hotel. St. John is considerably different from when I was there in 1941 or earlier. There are super-highway bridges in the reversing falls area, although there appears to be a park there, but we didn't go. The hotel, the Delta Brunswick, was located on King Street, near where Uncle George had his paint shop. We arrived at the reception desk, and were able to get a room for the Hayes'. I don't know whether they would have chosen such a place, but it was not very expensive, and the rooms were nice ($69). We drove up on the parking deck, carried our luggage in, and parted until dinner. Mary Ann and I walked around, and looked at my grandfather's house, which is now 6 apartments. The building in which the store was located has been razed, and the empty lot is used for

Museum in St. John, New Brunswick

parking. The old house still looks pretty good, and the plate glass panels in the front door are still there, but the neighborhood has substantially declined. Not far away, on Germain Street, the church and houses have been very well maintained.

We walked up toward King's Square, and the Loyalist Cemetary, and went in the fire department's museum. They were about ready to close, but I went in and saw a photograph of Fire Station #1, which was located half a block down Charlotte Street from my grandfather's store, and where I watched the horses come tearing out each noon with my grandmother. There were two young people attending the museum, college kids, part of a government program, who were nice, and torn between the desire to close up and the desire to have us visit the museum. The engine that I watched coming out of Station #1 was sitting in the main display room, its brass all polished and ready to go. There was a photograph upstairs of the men being drawn by horses on such an engine, but the higher-ups in the photograph had top hats on, which had been abandoned in the 30s. The protective helmets worn by the hose men were as I remember them. Mary Ann asked the young man where a good place to have dinner would be, and he recommended Billy's, a fish restaurant next to the City Market. There was some kind of a music festival while we were there, and the band stand in King's Square was draped with streamers, and various performers and their support were milling around, and some street performers were playing raucously, but not in much of an organized nature. We went back to the hotel, paused briefly to pick up the Hayes', and back up the street to the restaurant. We were seated in a window table, and after awhile had our dinners — I had broiled salmon and salad, the Hayes' had scallops and soup, and Mary Ann had seafood Newburgh. Our conversation was family-type, their son's girlfriend is a bartender and computer whiz, climbing up in some fast lane business.

As we ate a disturbance erupted at the next table. The old man who came in first was very aggressive, and he was joined later by four others, and our waitress told us later that they had asked that we be moved so they could have more room. They weren't excessively crowded. I decided later that they came in with no intention but to cause a disturbance and that they were French Canadians. We finished our supper, and commiserated with the waitress, and walked out for a brief tour of my grandfather's old neighborhood. Carroll very generously said that his father's old neighborhood had fallen into total disrepair. They had gone out in the afternoon and examined churches, and Carroll was taken with the St. John Synagogue, which is right there. The summer evenings linger on in the northern latitudes, and we turned into the hotel about 9:00 PM. The lobby was frothing with young people and Shriners, and later in the night they caused a disturbance, which escaped me, although Mary Ann knew about it.

August 13

We got up, showered, and decided to have breakfast before taking a walk.

After breakfast we went for a walk, down to the slip. We first had gone through the very attractive part of downtown St. John, only one street removed from Charlotte Street, and back up Duke Street to see my grandfather's house again. Then we walked back to Prince William Street, which is almost at the edge of the harbor, and read historical markers, one for a shipping company, and another for the great fire of 1877.

Mary Ann was beginning to get panicky — We wouldn't be able to get a taxi, we couldn't check out...we'd be late for our 9:30 AM bus to Fredericton, etc., so we went to our room, checked out rapidly, and got in the taxi poised at the head of the 4 taxi queue, put our 4 bags in his trunk, and slithered off to the bus station which was 4 blocks away.

We hopped out, bought our bus tickets, $16+/-, to Fredericton, along the St. John River. We had ¾ of an hour until departure, so we strolled out to re-examine the Loyalist Cemetery and King's Square. So far as I know, not a one of my ancestors is buried there, but there is absolutely no question that my guys knew those guys. We took a scenic bus trip along the St. John River to Fredericton.

We were let out at the bus station, and went up the hill to the university. The university overlooks the city, and the main building has a small university main building look. We went about 150 yards past the gate and were let out at Lady Beaverbrook Residence, which had a big Elderhostel banner above the entrance, so we knew we were in the right place.

The door was locked, and we were ready to go exploring when the coordinator, Lisa Cluff, came bounding up. She unlocked the door, gave us our keys, and led us to our rooms. The dorm was the first at U.N.B. Going to our room we crossed through a large common room, with a dining room adjacent, both furnished with very dark wood and a somber, academic look. Our room was quite nice, with a lavatory, and two widely-separated dorm spaces, and a fireplace, large windows, possibly the best dorm room on the campus. Our coordinator, Lisa, was a vivacious young lady, and when I asked, she said this was the first Elderhostel with which she had been associated. Earlier in the summer she had coordinated a camp for very young children, and I told her that was the best training for coordinating Elderhostlers. She gave us directions for walking to the center of Fredericton, about a mile away, and we started off.

At the gate of the campus there is a stoplight, and you must cross a busy road. In Nova Scotia and New Brunswick the pedestrian has the right-of-way, but for someone who has spent his life in states where there is not the law it is difficult to act like the natives. I like to be certain the car is going to stop before I step in front of it. At the intersection in question there is a pedestrian signal and a button to activate it. So we finally mastered this corner and walked down University Street, first through an area with support enterprises, a convenience store...and then past successively grand dwellings, early 20th century to Victorian.

Statue of Robert Burns, Fredericton, New Brunswick

Crossing Rte. 102, we reached the river edge park that is an important feature of downtown Fredericton. It is ½ mile long+/-, and there are running paths, and dog walkers, children walkers, elderly, etc. At the end of the park there was a statue of Robert Burns, but he was never here.

Then came the Beaverbrook Museum of Art, which had been the high point of my visit many years ago. We didn't go at the time — Too busy with genealogy. The Assembly for N.B. is across the street, and various provincial office buildings are spaced along the street, and a large hotel, until you come to the cross street which leads to the new bridge. We negotiated the tricky crossing in two stages, and made our way into the courtyard of the officers' barracks, which is a handsome old building, dating to 1839, and looked at the Beaverbrook statue and peeked in the gift shop where Mary Ann got a couple of postcards, and we decided to postpone seeing the museum.

When we got back we had our first meeting with Robert Fellows, the lecturer on genealogy in the Provincial Archives which was located about

50 yards up the street from the dorm. He introduced us to the facilities. A big percentage of the archives have been put out on microfilm. Many things are indexed, and in ordinary books, by the name of the individual in most cases. So a good rule is to use the indices before you tackle the microfilm. There are also many short mimeographed articles, filed next to the entrance to the reading room. Also, the professional archivists are there all of the time, ready to help. I found them extremely helpful. I got some of the documents, and started looking at some indices for Queens County. Then it was dinner time.

We finished dinner and went back to the dorm, where Lisa had us introduce ourselves, etc. The group seemed elderly, but that has been my initial reaction to each of the Elderhostel groups I have been in, and when it comes time to part, they seem younger. Then to bed.

August 14

We got up at 6:30 AM. We walked up the hill to the dining hall, about ¼ mile, and there is a fine view from outside just before you get there, and another through the huge window (30 ft. high) in the main room of the dining hall, but not the new superhighway bridge, and the main feature is a mile or so of the river and its lush surroundings.

We ate breakfast, and I had a brief conversation with the woman who had annoyed me the night before which went something like this:

> Her—"When I was in Ireland I was surprised to learn St. Patrick was Anglican, not Catholic."
>
> Me—"No, no, that's the whole point...When St. Patrick built the bonfire on The Hill of Slane, all of the people from miles and miles around came and were converted to Catholicism, and the Irish don't want to renounce, even to this day."

Her—"It depends on who you listen to."

At that point I was speechless. Mary Ann had lectured me not to get angry at the elderly, that there isn't much hope at stomping out ignorance and misconception in this group, and stupidity is incurable at any age. Somehow I managed to avoid the woman for the rest of the week.

Next was the class entitled "Internet for the Interested." Mary Ann thought she was not computer literate enough for this, and I thought that if the Internet was to be seriously probed, that it would be out of reach for her. She skipped the first class, and walked on the campus, up to the adjacent campus of St. Thomas, a university with a symbiotic relation with the U of NB, the latter being scientific- and forestry-oriented, and the former a Catholic institution with a social science and humanities leaning. She also went to the book store and bought a pad of paper and some postcards.

In the class, the instructor, Jack Gallagher, showed us how to log in, and he had arranged for dummy accounts in a LAN (Local Area Network) so the Elderhsotlers could send letters to each other. His software was called Quest, and everyone who attended was quite pleased. Jack's teaching approach was very laid back; we were seated at computers in a room in Head Hall, and he strolled among us, trouble shooting, and getting people started. I had the impression that the server was not very big — We were unable to learn we had been accepted in the remote dummy account until the next day.

The next class, at 10:30, was conducted by Bob Fellows, the archivist who was lecturing on NB Family History. Mary Ann joined me, and his lecture covered the material in his orientation lecture the day before. It was time for lunch, and we walked up the hill again to McConnell Hall and had our slightly better than average dorm lunch.

We went back to the dorm for a little bit, then walked up to the

University of New Brunswick

main library. The entrance foyer is a large room, and there are 10 or so terminals to use the online catalogue. Then we were led down the hall to a conference room, where there were 30 or 40 chairs set up, and a lot of books on tables, which were a good sample of books from the library of potential use to our group. I grabbed one book, *Loyalist Lineages of Canada*, and found the Van Warts right away. The research librarian, Kathryn Hilder, explained the holdings of the library, which is one of the best for United Empire Loyalists in the world. The library has a million books, including microfilms. Mrs. Hilden is collaborating with a professor of history in a book about a regiment which marched from Fredericton to Quebec to Kingston in the dead of winter in 1815 without a loss of life (I think). The history professor divides his time between the University of Newfoundland and U.N.B., choosing the winter term in Fredericton.

I copied some stuff from two volumes, then ran upstairs to photocopy a page from an index to the land petitions. There were 15 Van Wart citations on the page. I was beginning to think that Jacob Van Wart was important (b.1730, d.1801), and copied his entry from one of the books.

After a while we went back over to the (Provincial) Archives, and I photocopied a 10 page genealogical study from the file Van Wart, family history, which had the arrival (verified later) of my ancestor in 1662 in New Amsterdam. I didn't study this document until later. We worked until suppertime, ate, and decided to skip the tour of the campus.

I took Mary Ann to the computer lab and went through the stuff we had done the day before, sending messages to each other, log in, and stuff like that. Mary Ann thought it was fun, but e-mail to someone in the same room is a little beneath my dignity. Then we went home, and to bed.

August 15

We got up, 6:30ish, and to breakfast. We both went to the Internet class, then I delegated Mary Ann to go to Bob Fellows lecture while I went to the archives.

I started by looking at the Cadestral Map, No. 149, which indicated all of the original grants. My grandfather's farm is denoted Kings, Lot Kars 3, and 70 acres was granted to Tamberlane Campbell, and the grant included an island. Just glancing over the map I spotted two other grants, to Isaac Van Wart and John Van Wart, in the center of the area bound by the river, the Belle Isle Bay and Washamadoak Lake. They are Kings, Lots 2 and 3 Belualah. The lot immediately north was granted to Jacob Pidgeon, and I grabbed on this because one of our family legends is that mother was in high school with Walter Pidgeon, the movie star ("Mrs. Miniver," etc).

Then I looked in several indices. Mary Ann met me for lunch, which we ate, and I sat beside Bob Fellows, and tried to apologize for skipping class.

In the afternoon I worked on indices of censuses, of land grants, of vital statistics, etc. By this time I was beginning to sense the nature of my problem. The Van Warts in New Brunswick are descendants of Jacob Van Wart, b. 1730 Tarrytown, N.Y. He had 8 children, and several of them had lots of children, and so on. The early records tend to be sparse, but as time went on got more inclusive. So by the 1871 censuses, there were scores of Van Warts, located in several different places. From the other end, I knew quite a bit about my grandfather, his farm, his store, etc., but I didn't know how to connect his line back. Equally, I wanted to fit Phoebe Ann Dykeman into the picture.

I came in at suppertime and located her up on the second floor of the search room. She worked hard on my genealogy, and toward the end of the week found numerous direct references to my relatives. She said it was fun, finding things especially, and she was more patient copying things down than I. We didn't duplicate very much, and between the two of us had a good background to the nature of the problem.

We ate dinner, downstairs now with the mob, good dorm fare.

After dinner we went to the Forestry Building, near the dining hall, entering by the wide front stairs to an entrance hall with a big display which says "One out of every four jobs in New Brunswick is forestry related." Then upstairs to a classroom. The teachers of our class wanted us in a circle, and we helped rearrange the furniture, tables and chairs, so this could be. Soon the rest of the class filed in, 10+/- who were interested in the Indians of New Brunswick. The teachers, Dave Perley and his wife Imelda were full-blooded Maliseets, and at the spearhead of the effort to protect and spread the culture of this group. Mary Ann was particularly taken with Imelda, an attractive, 40ish, mother, in the late stages of getting an advanced degree at the university, and becoming a Medicine Woman in her tribe (p.c. nation). Dave lectured first on the Mic Macs and Maliseets, the Indians of the area. He spent some time explaining the proper way to talk about Native Americans, and then located their concentrations on the map, spoke about the larger confederation (Algonquin) to which they belonged.

Then we all got in a circle, and each person spoke his mind. This was organized by passing an eagle feather around the circle. You could talk when you held the feather, as long as you liked, and no one could interrupt. Then you passed to the next person. It is a civilized custom. Mary Ann was glad to be here, and I said I had a good friend who is a Cherokee. Then Imelda talked about the Maliseet language, her efforts to get stories in the language, and similar things. She has classes with children all over the province, in which she tells them to speak the language with their grandparents, etc. At the end we passed the eagle feather around again, and everyone spoke their minds. I tried to enter the spirit of an Indian circle and said: "I would like to tap into the power of the elderly" (a concept Imelda had introduced when she talked, saying, more or less, "I feel the power of elderly wisdom in this circle."). Frank Tabey said music was a good remark because it was short and said something. Then we went back to the dorm and to sleep.

August 16

We got up as usual, and walked up the hill to breakfast, mixing with the youngsters, trying to figure out how to get toast, coffee, ice water, clean knives and forks, and seats conveniently located among our fellow Elderhostlers. As it gets towards the end of a week, you have mastered these things, and it is time to move on to a new line, new customs,...

This morning I talked with Jo Lynam, one of the genealogical resource consultants, and her father had a wholesale grocery business on the slip at the foot of King Street in St. John, and we agreed that her father and my grandfather knew each other. We walked down to the Internet class and Jack had us in Windows, and onto the U.N.B. announcement page. I went to the online catalogue for the library and got 117 books on the subject search for United Empire Loyalists and New Brunswick. I read through the list of titles, relatively rapidly, but it still took a while. Mary Ann was next to me, and needed some help with Windows conventions, but she was able to do some things.

So off down the street, half the morning wasted. I walked through the middle of the St. Thomas campus going back, in the midst of the arriving band campers, with their instruments and their parents. I got some smiles.

I walked back a considerably different way. We had dinner, which helped, located the post office, but Mary Ann was reluctant to drop her cards into an unmarked slot in the wall, so she didn't.

Mary Ann was feeling upbeat. She had located lots of Van Warts and Dykemans in the indices, and was getting some references without having to read microfilm.

The evening class in Indian Life was conducted primarily by a medicine man, a chief of the Maliseets.

Then we walked back, to bed.

August 17

We got up 6:30 AMish, and up the hill to breakfast as usual. By now we were pausing momentarily at the good views, and this morning there was a little mist on the river, a faint ribbon tracing its curve, obscuring the bridges, a different aspect entirely. At breakfast Jo Lynam came over, animated, and said, "I've solved all of your problems!" And then she went away to give similar news to another Elderhostler. I didn't really know what she meant at the time, but it turned out that it was not an overstatement. She gave me a slip of paper and two contacts: one, Jack Van Wart, from Fredericton, and the other a lady in the Gagetown area, Marie Jenkins (whom we did not contact, unfortunately). I was to call Jack after 1:00 PM. Ms. Lynam was not going to be back. She said she had been able to help people this much before, but never so rapidly. She also told us to go to a bed and breakfast called Broadview, about 10 km south of Gagetown, where we were planning to go once the Elderhostel program ended.

After breakfast I asked Lisa how to use the telephone to get a reservation, and she offered to do it for me, sweet girl. Then we went to computer class, in which Jack showed us how to use the UNB Internet browser. I asked Jack if he could put me into my server (alpha) in Athens, which we had tried unsuccessfully on Monday, and in about 30 seconds there I was. I checked my mail, got hung up trying to reply to a letter in elm, switched to the e-mail software pine, and sent e-mail to all my Athens buddies. It is truly a strange feeling to be using the server in Athens from Fredericton.

After computer class, I attended Bob Fellows' class on genealogy, while Mary Ann went to the archives. His hour and a half lecture, which was folksy, anecdotal, and contained some theory of archiving often not easy to extract. He had a long list of reasons why a person might be interested in genealogy. Also he urged the members of the class to keep journals, which I have been doing for years on my vacations.

After class I met Mary Ann, so we could walk up to lunch together. She was excited, because she had found Phebe Ann Dykeman as a witness in two weddings, in 1847 in Waterborough and in 1852. The weddings were those of her sisters, Julia Ann and Sarah Mariah. Mary Ann had copied a lot of Van Wart census material, which now I consider valuable in contributing to the whole picture, and fleshing out the history of the

Van Warts and the area. Mary Ann was more patient than I at this point.

At lunch we mingled and compared successes with members of our group, and the band kids gave a short concert, which improved dramatically as they went along. When they finished, they quickly stashed their instruments and got in the cafeteria line. So much for art.

Much later we climbed the hill for dinner, figuring to go to the Indian class afterward. I called Jack Van Wart, and quickly learned the names of my ancestors. I called Mary Ann so she could make notes. It was exciting to have my genealogical dilemmas resolved so dramatically. He said he would prepare some material for me, but he wanted to tell me some things over the phone so I could make good use of my time before I talked to him in person. We agreed to meet Sunday at 2:00 at his house. He told me that my mother's mother's mother was Phebe Ann, which resolved my Phebe Ann Dykeman problem, as mother had told us the sampler was her grandmother's. I was trying to find her as her father's mother, and obtaining only difficulties, not the least because Phebe/Phoebe was a common name in the censuses. It hadn't sunk in how much difference this new information had made to my genealogical search. I had pursued reasonable lines of inquiry until the problem appeared almost intractable. I needed a totally new idea. Jack's connection caused the whole picture to clarify. This is exactly what happens when a good mathematical problem is solved. In a narrow sense, Jack handed me the answer. But from the mixed genealogical-historical point of view, what was going on in that part of the world, and what role my family have in it all, his considerable information was the precipitating agent.

Following this 15 minute phone conversation we went up the hill to our final Indian class. I went to sleep, and Mary Ann watched a video.

August 18

We got up, climbed the hill for breakfast, ate with our fellows, and came back to the dorm to learn that the computers were down in Head Hall. I worked on the journal, reviewed the genealogical results, and prepared to go to the archives at 10:00 AM when they opened. I got the archivist to help me get photocopies of the Cadastral Map sections with the portions with my grandfather's farm and the grants to John Van Wart and Isaac in 1828+/- on them. Meanwhile Mary Ann was making major progress with the censuses. She found my great-grandfather's (David Van Wart) family listed in the 1851, 1871, 1881 censuses (located in Kars, Kings) and another great-grandfather, NB Cottle, listed in 1861 in Cambridge, Queens, and Phebe, age 33, Charity, age 2, in his household.

We went outside, and then back to the university by a slightly different route, past the Anglican Church with the new copper almost completely installed on the spire by now, five days after we first saw it. Mary Ann steered me up the university street, and we passed some high school age girls, also on their way back to the dorm. We got back to the dorm just in time to change for the banquet.

The banquet was held in the room in the dining hall which we had abandoned the first night. There was a cash bar, and I talked to Kathryn again, and asked her what I should do with my mathematics books, and she made some suggestions which were not very useful. One, that I give them to Bosnia, does not at the moment seem very wise; like throwing them in a black hole. Then I talked to Shirley Deale, the recently-divorced psychiatrist from Portland, who is lonely but recovering. We had place cards in the dining room, the tables arranged banquet style, with me adjacent to Frank Tobey and Mary Ann next to Imelda's mother, and a Mohawk woman next to her.

Later we repaired to the dorm in the common room, and Lisa's father fiddled. He is possibly the best fiddler I have ever heard in a small group like this (as opposed to a violinist). He was self-taught, ordering his first fiddle from a catalogue when he was 12. His brother was his accompanist over the years, but he died recently, at which point he chorded while he played tunes we know, like "Turkey in the Straw," and "Red Wing." About half of the bunch got up to dance, led by two Indian women who danced Indian-style. I had the impression they were all familiar with folk dancing. Mr. Cliff played for about 20 minutes, and then I read mother's poems again. Technically my presentation was a little better – the room had very good acoustics. The effect wasn't quite so good. Anyway, they clapped, and when I sat down Shirley said thank you, which was much appreciated by me. Frank then introduced in a lengthy way a Czech song which he sang for us, and there weren't any other performances, so Mr. Cliff played for another thirty minutes, with Lisa accompanying. Then our entertainment broke up, and we went to bed, about 30 ft. down the hall.

August 19

We got up for our last breakfast, scrambled eggs, not so many youngsters when we got there. Not many of this bunch were going onto another Elderhostel. Lisa offered to take me to the hotel to pick up my rental car. I went into the Sheraton, and there were two boys at the car rental desk, and there I got bad news about the mileage surcharge.

The second boy took me out to the car, a bright red Pontiac Starfire, with 2,000 kilometers on it. Then on through the scrub growth, finally back to the river. Our B & B was below Gagetown. After lunch we went across the street to the Tilly Museum, where the student tour guide was in 1850s period dress. I remember the stereopticon, much like the one at my grandfather's farm. At the end I was given a copy of my

Gagetown Ferry

mother's mother's father's (Nathaniel Cottle) will from 1806.

We went out and caught the Gagetown ferry. The ferries here are very good, and free. There is a cable across the river, and the ferry threads it through its engine. In 1935 you could see the steel cylindrical rollers on the cable, but on the modern version all of this is out of sight. They are also much faster and busier. Sometimes in 1935 it would be almost half a day before someone came along. I told him my grandfather was John Van Wart, and he said, "There are Van Warts all over." Then he hopped back in to bring us safely to the other side. We drove around Washamadoak Lake, a beautiful and almost completely unspoiled area.

We went back over and reached the Broadview B & B about 4:00 PM. We drove up a steep hill to the house, past a sign which said, "Welcome from Bob and Mildred" with a big barn adjacent, parked the car and went inside. A young woman came out from the kitchen, and we said we had reservations to stay overnight, and she said to go on up and choose a room. This seemed rather informal to me. We chose the blue room in front. I took a nap, and Mary Ann read in the alcove in the hall.

We went down to the front porch, which has a spectacular view over two or three branches of the river and Washamadoak Lake. Two groups of diners came in, and soon we noticed that the hanging baskets and sugar water feeder were a hive of activity from the hummingbirds. After dinner we went out on the porch, and Bob came by and we had a lengthy conversation, in which we learned he had had a heart attack ten years ago, and that was when and why they opened the B & B.

They ran a thriving business, serving 179 diners on Mother's Day. Then, when I told him where my grandfather's farm was, he told me that his mother had grown up in that house, only leaving in 1931 when she got married (another revision to my family legend that my grandfather had sold the farm in 1923).

He called up his mother and verified some of the details. We went to sleep.

August 20

We woke up with the sunrise, a nearly full moon visible out over our window. After breakfast we went the ten or twelve miles down to Evandale, where we got on the ferry. The ride across the river takes 5 minutes at most, but that gave us time to get out of the car, and look both up and down the river. The ferry holds at most 4 cars now in a single file. My grandfather's house itself is little changed from 1935, but the setting has been overwhelmed by the building of a huge maintenance shed for the ferries. I think it may be the main shed for all of them: Gagetown, Belleisle, Hampstead, Upper Gagetown, and Evandale. It is at most 100 feet from the house, across the road.

When we got there, we parked the red car, and knocked at the back door, but everyone was gone. They had a big, old-fashioned cold drink chest in the area behind the back door, suggesting an attempt to provide drinks to those using the bathing float down in front. But the float was in a reedy area, which must be a happy home for eels, as it was in 1935. Mary Ann and I walked back over the big field behind the hill, from which John had taken his 1935 pictures. It was in hay now. There was a big deer stand on top of the hill. The high tension line is there, going across the river between the two houses, Grandfather's and the Jones'. We spent ¾ of an hour, found another deer stand approximately where I had made a lean-to and little bridge in 1938, I suppose. We then drove up to the road. I wanted to see Tennant Cove, a small cove south along the river, which was one boundary of my grandfather's farm. There was a large sign for the cemetery.

We parked and went down, and they were all Van Warts, going back to my direct ancestors, Mary Fowler Van Wart, wife of Jacob Jr. (died in 1851, aged 92) and John and Hannah (Gerow). Jacob Jr. is buried there, but there is no stone. It was a beautiful sunny morning, and I sat on the grass and copied the epitaphs, the last line of Mary's being illegible. The stones were very nice, with elaborate rosettes on the two oldest. The cemetery has stones from then until now, perhaps 50 in all, about half of them Van Warts. But they are my distant cousins, I know now, descendants of John and Hannah. The only distracting note was the firing from the range.

We wanted to be in Fredericton at 2:00 PM, to keep our appointment with Jack. So we turned around and retraced our steps, finally getting to Fredericton about 1:00 PM. We drove to Jack's house, on Brunswick Street, only 5 minutes late, and he was waiting and motioned me to park in the driveway. In some sense I recognized him — There was a family resemblance. I jumped out and shook his hand, a little excited. I forgot to introduce Mary Ann, but they introduced themselves while I got my treasures from the car. He invited us in, and Anna, his wife, was there, suggesting that we go to the sun room to talk. We talked a mile a minute for about an hour, comparing our lives, and filling in genealogical blanks for each other – my contribution being facts about my grandfather, and my own family.

He first showed me 10 pictures from the Isaac Erb collection of photographs made between 1901-1910, I suppose, which are on glass now. About 5 of those are of Grandpa Van, and Uncle George and Willy Peterson are in three or four of them. My Great Uncle Danny is definitely on one. Then we went to the dining room, and Jack went upstairs and brought down an enormous amount of genealogical material he had prepared for me – two pages of ledger paper with my direct line back to Holland, 9 generations, which he had done by hand since I first got in touch with him, as well as 10 or 15 photocopied pages from his records. These included all of my direct Van Wart ancestors.

Jack and Anna's house is a museum – they have beautiful old paintings and prints, and artifacts of one sort or another, closely packed into his father's house, a white frame steep-roofed turn of the century structure, two or three blocks from downtown Fredericton, on a street on which major government skyscrapers (9 story) are located three blocks away. His backyard is an elegant garden in late August, and we sat there for a while. We had high, loud communication every minute of the 2½ hours we were together. I tried to present myself accurately, but pushed ahead too rapidly once or twice, not taking into account his point of view, something that would have been obvious to me with a moment's reflection. But that characterized my week in Fredericton.

He did genealogy because he enjoyed it at the time — Perhaps he was an unrequited scholar — And the source of information was at hand, and perishable. I hope he can pass it on, possibly to the benefit of his children. He pointed to a spot in his dining room in which he remembered that Aunt Della had stood during his wedding.

At about 5:00 PM we got up to leave, and Jack went upstairs to get me the address of the current owners of the Isaac Erb negatives, so I could get some for myself. He was gone more than 5 minutes (entering things in his records while they were fresh, I believe), while we stood with Anna in the front hall. Jack told me he had had two heart attacks, but he looked healthy, not heavy, and something like my grandfather. Once or twice, as we talked rapidly, I had the feeling I was talking to myself. It was more the pace of understanding, the rhythm of the mind, together with a faint family resemblance, that made me feel that way. We said goodbye, and drove down to the parking lot, to go into town to make arrangements for our night's lodging.

We walked down Queen Street and saw the entrance to the museum at the Officers' Barracks doubled as the Tourist Information station. We got some change, and then the young lady there very nicely called the B & B we had chosen from the list, and made a reservation for us.

We sped out of town following our directions to Appelot, our B & B. Over the bridge, follow Rte. 105 along the river for 14 km. Even good, explicit directions involve some anxiety, but as the car registered 14 km. there we were, and we drove up the hill, and were met by our hostess, Elsie Myshrall, a slender blonde woman, who showed us our room. The bathroom, though small, was ours.

We went upstairs, showered, and went to bed.

August 21

In the morning we went down to breakfast at 7:30 AM, and sat down on the porch. I had eggs, sunny side up, and Elsie said that's what French Canadians ate. Everything was very good, and I sat facing the window on the porch, overlooking the St. John River, to a large island, with big fields and a barn, etc., about ¼ mile away. Then I saw a big bird moving along the bank of the opposite side of the river, black but also with a pronounced flash of white, and I said, "I think that's an eagle." Elsie got some glasses, and called her granddaughter, who confirmed for me – "That's an eagle all right." He went in a tree on the bank and sat there, and you could see that he was white from the neck up, and had a yellow beak. We had him in sight for two or three minutes while he worked the edge of the river. That was my first eagle in the wild, and I was beside myself.

We got off the Trans Canada Highway at a sign for Jemseg, and worked our way through some construction, and it was not clear whether we were there or not, when we saw some youngsters scraping paint off a building next to a church. So I stopped the red car, got out and asked if they could direct me to the cemetery for the church, and they said, "Oh, it's just down the road." I asked if it was an old cemetery, and they said yes. So we drove down the road about ¼ mile, and into a field, and I walked straight to the grave of Phebe Ann Cottle, beloved wife of Deacon N. B. Cottle, my great-grandmother and great-grandfather. Most of the people buried there were Dykemans. The oldest date of birth was for my great-great-grandfather, Deacon Nathaniel Cottle, born in 1794. (I think he was the oldest, though there were stones that looked older.) A little later we learned that this was the Baptist Dykeman cemetery, and that the Baptists and Anglicans split in the 1830s. I copied the inscriptions while Mary Ann searched for other possible graves with names of my relatives, but she didn't locate any.

Then we went across to Cambridge Narrows, along Washamadoak Lake, which is beautiful. We decided to stop again at the Eveleighs, if we could. It was directly on our way to the airport.

About 3:30 PM we went in again, and were able to get a room. Mildred said we would have to eat at 7:00 since her husband had to go to the doctor the next day, and they had to leave early. There were two soldiers standing by a jeep, and we learned that they had just had a bath upstairs. She said that this was one time only. There are several thousand soldiers training in the large military base there, preparing to assist in the pullout of Bosnia, three thousand U.S. troops among them.

We went upstairs, and I napped for a short while. Then we went down and sat on the porch, and I saw an osprey out in the broad-view, recognized by his behavior as much as his markings. He took off from the edge of the water, and in practically no time was miles away, almost straight up.

Then we went in to dinner. There were 5 ladies there, and before too long it was clear that it was Bob's mother, who had lived in my grandfather's house from 1922 until she got married in 1931, she said. She was married there. After they had finished, we talked for 15 or 20 minutes, and I told them what I could remember from my stays there. Her father raised garden vegetables, and she and her sister did the weeding. Her sister was a slight woman with an intelligent look in her eye. I told them about visiting the Jenkins, and being given a pole to fish with, and losing the only fish that had taken my bait.

Then they told me that one day they fished the whole length of the creek, and walked home from the end. They said they went to parties over on Tennant Cove, and they boys walked them home in the dark. Bob had invited them to dinner so we could meet them, I am certain. One of the other ladies was a niece of Maud Jenkins, who was a Van Wart, a fact I had forgotten. Both women became animated when they talked about the old days. The other ladies were somehow related to them, one a daughter, and the other a cousin perhaps. Bob's mother and her sister were in their 80s.

We showered and went to bed.

August 22

We saw the sunrise again, and got down to breakfast at 6:55 AM, consistent with our promise, and were packed and ready to go by 7:30.

The Eveleighs saw us off, and we weren't more than a mile or two down the road when they passed us in their station wagon, headed for St. John, I suppose. We crossed the river at Evandale, and drove to the farm of Roy Jones, whose farm was next to my grandfather's. He was standing outside the back door, and there was a litter of kittens which he may have been feeding. He had a big hat on, and was an old man in his eighties. He invited us in, and brought out his treasures. The first was the original grant for the property his farm was on, complete with a 5-inch diameter bees wax seal attached by a ribbon. Then he showed me the Cadastral map from which I had gotten photocopies, and two books, the first I had seen in our library, and the second with two photographs of my grandfather's store. I got information about this publication, to see if I could find a copy. He told us that my grandfather's house was built in 1909-10, that Bill Peterson came up to change it from duplex to single dwelling. He said his grandfather helped remove the cannons from the Eagle's Nest, the fortified point down the river from our farm.

I always believed it was a very old fort, but now believe it was put in during the War of 1812, when the British thought the U.S. might raid. We were in his kitchen, and he had a blazing fire in the stove, and it was quite warm and smoky in there. Someone came to the door, and I thought we should go in. It was a young man campaigning for the upcoming Canadian election. He told Roy he was a distant relative. We snuck out the back door, and waved goodbye, and shook hands with the candidate and wished him luck.

When I got back I turned the car in, and we checked in our bags. There was a 12-year-old boy being put on the plane by his grandmother and grandfather. Our plane to Toronto was more than ¾ filled. The snack was better than the last couple of snacks we'd had. Pretty soon we were in Toronto, checked through customs, missing the Duty Free shop, making certain we got to our flight on time.

We boarded the Air Canada flight to Atlanta, and were home in a couple of hours. We had three hours in the Atlanta airport before our shuttle left, so we had a small supper there. I decided to try and exchange my Canadian money, but got to the window just as she closed it. I went outside and met Mary Ann at the shuttle bay, and in a few minutes it drove up, the driver being one of Mary Ann's clients. We came home and went to bed.

TAHITI

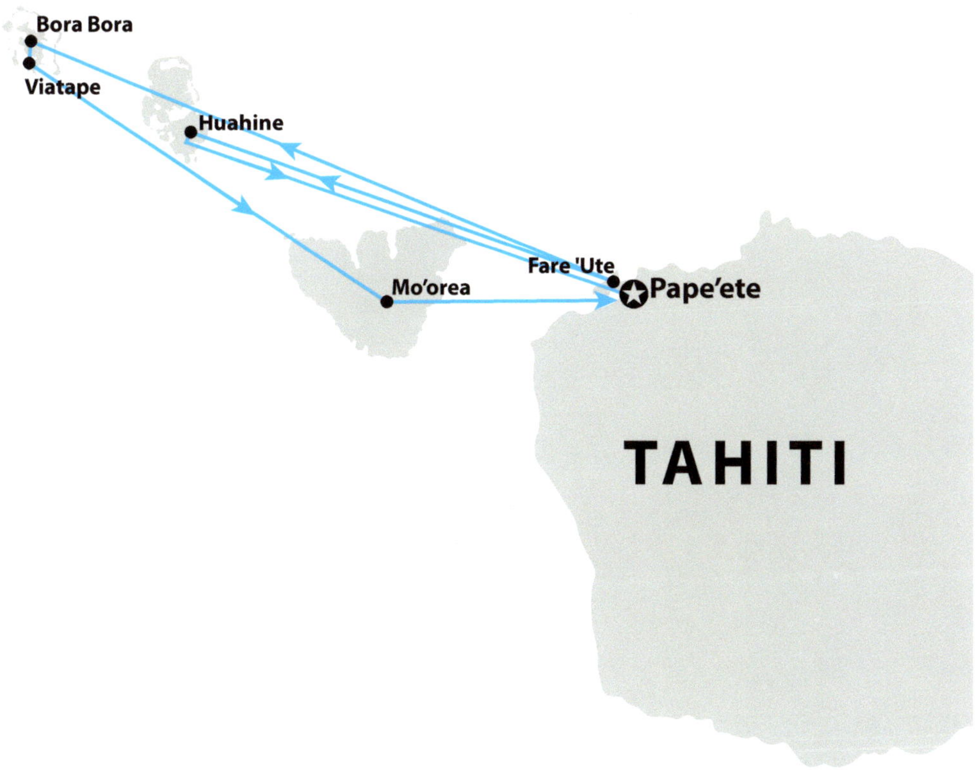

Bora Bora
Viatape
Huahine
Fare 'Ute
Mo'orea
Pape'ete
TAHITI

There is much to admire in the Polynesian culture. Obtaining food was not difficult: there were plenty of coconuts and fish were abundant in the lagoons. They lived family-style – the care of children was communal.

There was a survival realization that new genes were necessary, leading to the friendly acceptance of strangers. The French colonization left its mark, but underlying it all is the Polynesian heritage.

Tahiti

August 24, 1997

I HAVE WANTED TO GO TO TAHITI SINCE I READ *TYPEE* WHEN I WAS VERY YOUNG, PROBABLY 13 OR 14. Our plans were made three months or more ago, and I have been reading about the South Pacific since then. I'm a professor by trade, so research calms me, but Tahiti was truly another world.

We landed at LAX, having come from Atlanta, and after some travail, we got to Air New Zealand flight to Tahiti. Our fellow passengers were more French than anything else, Polynesians second, some elderly English, Australian and New Zealander couples, and three or four honeymooners. We got on the plane. As we left LA we could see two islands. We were on the right side of the plane, and as we headed southwest into the Pacific, we prolonged the sunset…it must have been an hour or more. It was orange and red at first, and extended as far as we could see out of our little window with the more intense shade of bright orange right in the middle, the direction of the sun itself. *It was like a heated sword blade across the horizon, slowly darkening.* It seemed we would never leave it, but we did, and it got dark.

About midnight, their time, we landed at Pape'ete. We didn't sleep long.

August 25

We waited a while, and the sun came up, and lit up Mo'orea across the lagoon for us. There were a few low grey clouds, and patches of light moved around us on the mountain, and the lagoon was turquoise, bordered by the white line of breakers, and the deep blue beyond. The outline of the mountain is distinctive, known to me from my postage stamps.

The workers were all Polynesian: very attractive, very calm people. After breakfast we walked down to Maeva Beach, to just beyond the hotel property, and there was a little coral there, and we could see lots of little tropical fish. Soon we were off, down to the lobby at 9:00 AM to be picked up for our 10:30 flight to Huahine at the Faa Airport.

The ride to the airport was through the industrial section of Pape'ete: tires, plumbing, nurseries. Mary Ann didn't think it was paradisical. We saw the local bus, called the truck, and lots of other traffic on our two mile trip. Our driver got us out and into the line for our flight on Air Tahiti.

There were lots of Japanese tourists — One group of 20 or so being addressed by an earnest young tour guide. We saw one beautiful, elegantly dressed young Japanese girl accompanied by an elderly businessman, and we both, independently, decided she was a geisha, or perhaps what you can get if you answer an ad for a "traveling companion." This winter we got, unsolicited, a catalogue of catalogues in the mail, which contained descriptions of two catalogues from which you could order "traveling companions." I suppose the world-wide market for them is vigorous.

After a 30-minute flight we landed at Huahine, and were driven the 5 miles or so to the Sofitel Maeva, through jungle vegetation some of the time, with the lagoon on the edge of the road – 20 feet away, from time to time. There was a road sign, "Children Playing," and sure enough in about 100 feet we came around a turn and there were two children playing, the younger without a stitch on.

We soon arrived at the gate of the hotel, de-vanned, and were greeted in the lobby by a pleasant young Polynesian girl, and a glass full of fruit juice. We know now she is the Entertainment Director, and we registered, which in the South Sea Islands includes the specifics of your departure plans. They don't want to encourage anyone to jump ship and "Go Native," and I can see why. The urge is strong.

We went to our bungalow, and after some minor unpacking, I got out my snorkel, mask and fins, and went to consult with the young Polynesian who was manning the aquatic booth to ask for advice. He said there was good snorkeling just after the last bungalow. He called it an underwater garden. And it was.

Bungalow in Huahine

The temperature of the water was perfect, and before long I saw some rocks under the water. I saw four or five different kinds of fish, tiny, 6 or 8 inches long. I swam around the coral for about twenty minutes or so, getting used to my gear. It was never very deep, 3 or 4 feet, but enough for snorkeling. There was a lot of coral, brain and otherwise. I came in before I'd really had enough. I tried to sleep, but I was too excited. So I went on the porch and worked on this journal. It is an excellent place to journalize, with the mountain across the lagoon.

We were both hungry, and we were lured to the cabin area by the drumming, Mary Ann said they were giving some kind of instruction, and when we got there it turned out to be hula dancing. Then we went in to dinner, and were seated by our entertainment director, who had a big flower arrangement in her hair, mostly in the back. We had a choice of beef or fish, and chose fish...because it's Tahiti. It was a fillet of some fairly large fish, in a good sauce, with spinach and a Polynesian vegetable. We had been almost the first to be seated, so we had to dawdle substantially to keep our seats for the entertainment, which was hula-hula dancing. The musicians played chants, and six girls danced, joined by three or four young men from time to time.

In the biography of Melville I read, the books of Melville were described as a big hit in America, eventually an influence in drawing society away from the Victorian stiff-collar way of describing behavior, then in vogue. There is no possible interpretation of the hula that isn't erotic, and the smiling girls dancing away near us were erotic, hitching down their skirts from time to time after some vigorous shaking caused them to hike up. But there was nothing in this performance that couldn't be shown to a child. While they were resting one of the young men did a fire dance. We learned later he was a Marquesan (from a nearby island chain), with considerable tattooing on one side of his body.

August 26

In the morning we got dressed and went to breakfast. *A long, leisurely breakfast, drinking more coffee than one should, looking out over the lagoon, with*

the breakers just visible on the reef, the terns cruising overhead, is clearly one of life's premier experiences.

I wanted to catch the 9:00 AM bus to the museum. Since I read how the anthropologists Marguerite and Kenneth Emory spent their honeymoon uncovering the exact same spot, I have wanted to see it. Most of their artifacts are reproductions. The explanations are enough that you can reconstruct what the archeologists believe to be true, and the displays make sense on several levels. There was a sign at the door, "Please take off your shoes." We saw a sequence of fish hooks (reproductions) and an explanation of the fish hook method of dating, which together with linguistics helped determine the time sequence of Polynesian settlement. Other things were used, of course.

I talked with the girl in charge, La Fie Delord. Yosi Sinoto is the archeologist responsible for establishing the museum. He was in charge of the major archeological project which cleared the site in the late 1960s.

We were in the museum three quarters of an hour or so, and then we went outside to look at the marae. They are flat stones, placed upright, and arranged here so as to enclose a rectangular area. There are 54 of them in the general vicinity, placed probably over 100 yards. We walked slowly down the water's edge toward the fish traps. We had to go up to the road to avoid going into the front yards of houses being lived in, with a Polynesian dog lying right there. *Polynesian dogs are quite different in temperament from ours.* They lie around asleep, oblivious to passers-by. When we take our evening walk at home the dogs start barking furiously when we come within 100 feet of their lot-lines.

We got a very good view of the fish traps, which are currently being used to trap fish. They have been in use continuously for 500 years at least. There are several entrepreneurs along the road here, Polynesians doing Polynesian things, in their leisurely way.

We got back near the time when we were to catch the bus (van, really), and La Fie was standing outside. She told us her genealogy: a German father, a Chinese grandfather, on her mother's side. And obviously quite a bit of Polynesian. I said most people in the U.S. had different nationalities in their backgrounds. She said, "A melting pot…so is the South Pacific."

At eleven the bus came, headed the wrong way, to Fare. As we came back our driver gave us lots of little tidbits of information – among them – at the bridge there was a side plot commemorating the massacre of the French who landed in 1835+/-. The driver said, "My ancestors beat them that time, but they came back later and brought guns and beat us. That's life." He explained about the island profile looking like a reclining woman, who had eight children, each of whom founded a town on the island.

This afternoon we checked out a mask and snorkel for Mary Ann and she practiced a few minutes, and discovered that breathing through her mouth was possible after all. She saw lots of little fish, and I think she enjoyed it. I snorkeled a lot longer than the day before. The coral garden is indeed spectacular. You can glide along in 3 ft. to 5 ft. of water. You can thread your way down canyons, and alongside extensive patches, rarely out of sight of a few fish, then coming across bunches. Some of the little ones are not more than an inch – the larger up to 8 to 10 inches. *It is hard to describe the fascination of snorkeling – the floating suspended with a gliding, pulsating, three-dimensional fairy world down below.* Eventually one has to come in.

We tried to be a little late to dinner.

Later an older Polynesian gave a lecture in English. He was teaching us how to acquire and use coconuts. At the end of the lecture he brought us all into the cabana area by the swimming pool, where there was a hundred foot tall coconut tree with lots of coconuts on top, and he climbed up (in around only 20 seconds), and threw down a coconut. He put a wet cloth around his feet, for traction, and made progress in jumps, holding on with his hands, and propelling himself with his legs. I would say that he was shinnying, but the "jumps" were much bigger, five feet or so.

The entertainers gave things they made to the audience, and Mary Ann was given the market basket. I hope we can bring it home, through customs, plant control. Before I came, as I was summarizing in my mind the things that I had read, I thought of a great line for the journal. *Since the time the first European explorers came to the Pacific islands, they have been an anthropological laboratory, sometimes even a test tube.*

We went home to bed.

August 27

In the morning we got up and experienced the spectacular view across our lagoon. We repeated our elegant breakfast. The morning was beautiful, and we went down on the beach for a photo-op, but as we walked near the coral garden, we discovered that the beach was covered with ossified pieces of coral, broken off and washed ashore. Joan asked us to bring her shells, and Danny is into coral reef diving, so we started a new project, shipping a coral reef home.

When I was young and had some sense I had an iron clad rule – We weren't going to carry rocks home in our suitcases when we went traveling. But now, in go the rocks. Well, I trained with weights for this trip, 97 days carefully checked off, so I suppose a few nice coral specimens in the laundry should not dismay me.

Boat tour around Huahine Iti

Our activity was a trip around Huahine Iti in a thatched picnic boat, and a snorkeling experience. We had a perfect day, and as we sped along the changing profiles and changing colors were a total mind experience. I read the painter Gauguin's comments about the colors in this part of the world, and until one experiences it the words seem extravagant, but they are not. Now, the picture of his house in Noa Noa, the Paris of his day, was considered by the art critics to be the fantasy of an unstable mind, are things you can see here. I can understand that he didn't feel ready to try panoramic landscapes. Color photography has reached the stage of being able to capture this range, and the travel brochures are filled with pictures, but I think one is tempted to discount them. At any rate, the effect of the change of light on time, as one moves along in a rapidly-propelled outrigger canoe, is not something that can be approximated by a photograph.

We passed two Polynesian fishermen in a boat, and our guides talked to them, asking if they had caught anything, and the man in the boat held up a can of beer. Some things are universal.

In a little while our guide stopped the canoe – about 100 feet from each edge of the lagoon – and he said, "OK, you guys, here is your snorkeling experience," or words to that effect. Everyone was a little nonplussed (a word I don't often use), but it was fine with me, and I wanted to be first in the water, but I don't think I quite made it. I was bested by a second or two. It would have taken a 1st Base umpire to call it. The snorkeling was better than in the coral garden near the hotel, but not by an order of magnitude. I saw perhaps 10 species. The nicest thing was that it was deeper, and the sides of the coral build-up were 10-15 feet instead of two or three. My three snorkelings so far had been of increasing interest. It was one of the main reasons I had come here – the water is just right, my technique is improving, and there are still fish in the ocean.

Mary Ann and I hippity-hopped over the side to the lunch barge which had a long table down its length, a big wooden bowl with salad in the middle, lettuce and shredded carrot, sliced tomato. We were passed a huge tray with grilled tuna and beef in the European style. There was bread at our places, and pineapple and watermelon, beer, wine, and coffee, and, oh, yes, a potato wrapped in foil. The 15 of us ate about half of the meat, and when we were done, the guide who grew up on Huahine put the meat in a smaller metal container, hopped in the outrigger, and disappeared over the horizon. He came back in about 20 minutes, and Mary Ann asked where he had gone and he said he gave the meat to people in one of the villages.

It is wrong to waste food, an idea understood better in less-advanced societies.

We got back in the outrigger and we sailed near an imposing white house on an island, which our guide said belonged to one of the old families, the whole island belonged to them. They raise all sorts of crops, vegetables, and he dropped his voice and speaking only to us, added marijuana. We batted this around for a while. Then we went out toward the reef, where a Polynesian man was spear fishing. I asked if they got many fish, and he said yes, two or three in ten minutes. So the man became active, and the guides started giving "whoops," but I think it was a false alarm.

Then we went back to our pier and back to our bungalow.

August 28

The next morning we were scheduled to go to Bora Bora at 9:00 AM. So we went in to breakfast at 6:45 or so, and ate for two (meals – well meals and people – there were two of us).

While we were waiting for the van to the airport the man who climbed the coconut tree was sitting there, weaving coconut artifacts, offering himself for photo-ops. I told him there was a French Polynesian postage stamp with a man at the top of a coconut tree, the stamp from the 1920's. He said, "That was my grandfather." I said, "I always wanted to see the climbers. I didn't really believe men did that." He said, "Now you've seen it," and laughed. Another deep travel conversation that would have disappeared into the mist were it not for the faithful journal. We piled in the bus, and traced our way back to the airport. *It always amazes me how different the same drive looks after you have been somewhere, even if for only three days.*

The flight to Bora Bora is 20 minutes or so. The plane was almost completely filled, but we quickly landed on the strip built by the U.S. in World War II. It is out on the edge of the lagoon, we were given 15 minutes to walk to the ferry which would take us to Viatape, where we were to be met by our tour bus. We went up to the deck and saw the famous profile of Bora Bora for the first time from the lagoon. The three-year-old child of a Canadian couple was crying, and a Japanese lady said a few words to her, and she stopped. I was much impressed.

We de-ferried to the pier at Viatape and saw the Sofitel bus, and they transferred our luggage, and we rode ten or fifteen minutes to the hotel, where we were given flowers to put on our heads. Mary Ann's was made with red flowers, mine with white. There were about 10 of us, and we had to register, were given fruit juice, and shown to our bungalow by a young Polynesian girl, who came back shortly after having directed the last couple to their bungalow, walked just inside the door, grabbed a shell suspended there, and asked, "Do you know what this is?" Mary Ann said, "It looks like a shell," and added, "You have to pull this to turn the lights on."

We went to dinner, a sumptuous seafood buffet. After our buffet we went to our bungalow for sweaters, and then came back for the entertainment, provided by a Polynesian club.

Then the Polynesian children came out to do the hula, one as young as four, coached by one of their mothers. Earlier we had listened to a lecture about Bora Bora, most of the time spent on the U.S. presence here during WWII. There were photographs – one of a U.S. cruiser under the mountain, and another of Eleanor Roosevelt talking to the commanding officer, with a circle of GIs nearby. The U.S. troops left behind several hundred children, and their descendants can be seen all over the island now. There was one of the youngsters dancing who had light brown hair. So I am back to the question – Should one teach erotic dancing to 8 to 12-year-old girls?

The emcee performed a vigorous fire dance. His baton twirling was faster than the boy on Huahine, but he didn't take as many chances. After the program an 8-year-old gave Mary Ann his lei as we wended our way back to our bungalow.

August 29

We had our first breakfast on Bora Bora on Friday morning. We couldn't walk to Viatape until we finally figured out to check out the outrigger. This was a happy choice. We paddled the half-mile or so to the motu which belongs to the hotel. The wind is a factor, and while it wasn't a very stiff breeze, whenever we steered it hit us broadside and swung us around. We saw some people from the Park Royal, with about the same level of expertise as ourselves, and they were going in circles, and backwards, so I didn't feel too bad, even though it must have looked pretty funny to the casual Polynesian observer.

Later that morning we tooled around, and then returned for breakfast. *This has to be one of life's great experiences, watching the sun come up over a South Sea island, dawdling over an infinite breakfast, watching more fish than you can identify in the crystal water below.*

At 9:00 or a little later we were scheduled to feed the sharks. We went through the drill, got our slips which verified that indeed, this morning we were *probably* on the list. Yesterday, when we had not made the list, but this was a new day. We went out toward the reef for ten or fifteen minutes, and anchored by a pool our Polynesian guide got in the water with a big bucket of fish scraps, which he put in the water, a scrap at a time. In 10 minutes four black fin sharks came up, and ten of our bunch were snorkellers, so we got in the water. We were supposed to stay behind the guide, but it was not that easy , since the tide was coming in over the reef and drifting me forward. The sharks were six to eight feet long, weighed around 250 pounds each, and moved swiftly in the water. The guide book says they are not dangerous to humans.

Our guide says he can usually get 20 or so sharks, but that there were so many people out on the reef that the sharks were scared away. As much as anything I liked the shower of little fish that churned around our activity. We were in 6 to 8 feet of water and could see hundreds of our little lagoon fish within 10 or 15 feet. The 10 of us were in a line between the outrigger and the guide, and it was difficult to keep out of people's way. Several of them had cameras (the people, not the sharks), the throw-away underwater kind. We climbed back in, up the ladder and were off on our circle of Bora Bora. It was beautiful watching the light change on the famous profile, and on the other side the breakers on the reef. Our guide told us the names of two or three hotels, and a cluster of condominiums up the side of the hill, and he said the first belonged to Marlon Brando, the second to Jack Nicholson, and that you could buy one for half a million dollars.

We went around the island in an hour or so, and found a school of around 15 stingrays. The guide went in the water and fed them. Everyone was a little reluctant to get in, but on his urging the snorkellers hopped in, and I am glad I did. *The motion of a swimming ray is very interesting, sort of a sine wave on the boundary of a disk*. It doesn't look the same from above as it does head on. One of them brushed up against me, startling me a little, as the guide was lifting them up and turning them over to pop fish in their mouths. They were about 4 feet in diameter, with 3 foot tails, which have some venom that will give you trouble if you get hit in a break in the skin. I don't think I would like to embrace one the way the guide was. Then we climbed back in the outrigger, and delivered some of our passengers to a picnic area motu. We were back at our pier in about 10 minutes after stopping to let people off.

Three of the honeymooners on our tour sequence, including Todd and Laura, were at the next table. We finished about 9:00 PM, waited around out front and read the names of the famous people who had eaten there, including the Rockefeller who went missing, Ringo Starr, Goldie Hawn, and who knows who else. Finally we were driven back, about 15 km, and arrived at the hotel just in time for the entertainment, a higher level version of the one we had in Huahine. The dancers were more synchronized, and the band was larger. I liked the shaking girls, especially the one directly in front of us, who smiled all the time. Afterward we went home to bed.

August 30

Garden bungalow

Our transfer to Mo'orea was the next morning. After another sybaritic fish watching breakfast, same as yesterday, we went back to our garden bungalow, took a last look at the reef from our beach and the distant islands on the horizon, with the sun rising, and the clouds drifting along, and back to have our luggage on the porch by 8:00 AM. The ferry ride from Viatape to the airport was the reverse of our original delivery, and we had the intervening circle island tour to reinforce our study of the mountain profile, and merge this with sharks, rays and coral canyons. I talked to one of the young women on our schedule, and asked if she knew anything of the story of Cheyenne Brando, and she said only what she remembered from television news at the time. She told me, and it coincided with what I remembered, except that she said the young man who killed her boyfriend was Marlon

Brando's son, then in prison. It seems to me that the whole story was designed for Italian opera. Then we were put on the plane, and took off for Mo'orea.

In a few minutes we landed. Our bungalow is 50 feet from the beach, which looks across at Tahiti (the only hotel on the island to do so, a piece of information available to us from many sources). As we came down the beach we followed three tiny little birds, not in the book, like sparrows, which were feeding on the seaweed that marks high tide. There were some people on a bicycling device that propels them fairly rapidly in the water.

August 31

In the morning we had our (overeating) breakfast, and then arranged for our rental car, with Conchita, and the drill was interesting. We had to wait while she prepped the other guy's car. Then she did the paperwork for us, and took us out to a Fiat Panda, green, and it took her three minutes to get it started. It wasn't very much different from my Fiat of 1971, and brought back fond memories. We went back to our room, picked up the snorkeling gear, cameras and binoculars, and left on our day tour of Moore, going to the waterfall first. Fortunately Conchita had given us the key instruction for finding the road off – if you get to the hospital you have gone too far. So we got to the hospital, and went slowly back, and there was, among several choices, a narrow path/road that didn't clearly terminate in a carport. We tried it, and after about 100 feet there was a Polynesian woman walking down the road with a dog and a child, so we asked, "Waterfall?" and she pointed us on. The road was washed out and full of potholes, but the Fiat is dependable in the lowest gear, so we crept along for a mile or so, and arrived.

The young man attending the gate took our money and pointed us up the hill for our 30 minute walk. We passed two or three farms. *Things want to grow, and farming is more beating back the jungle than anything else.* If a coconut falls on a damp spot, in three weeks you have a young coconut palm growing away. They are weeds, and the biggest Tahitian predators for humans are coconuts falling on heads. We saw a huge one fall in the garden of the hotel as we walked along. There are coconuts ready-to-eat lying on the ground everywhere.

Beautiful Tahitian waterfall

As we walked along we could see the changes in botanical niche, from lagoon edge to first mountain level. The stream draining the waterfall was by our side, and we came by two very attractive pools that would have been fun to plunge in. After 20 minutes we reached an open spot, with enough room for two or three vehicles, they'd better be 4-wheel drive to have gotten there, and the path/road ended, to be replaced by a narrow foot trail. We went along this, Mary Ann in the lead, with one or two places where a person could get his Reeboks wet if he weren't prudent. There was 20 feet of stone steps as we neared the fall. It was spectacular when we got there – a thin fall of 300 ft.+/- down the back mountainside, into a pool, 50+/- inch diameter, and you can get down to it. We took photographs, paused five minutes or so, and headed back. On the trip down we met Todd and Laura, our neighbors in Huahine. They had heavy, well-worn hiking boots on, and I assured them that the trail ahead was without problems for people with such gear. I saw a red-browed waxbill, actually three of them, in a tree as we walked along. The farms are not very big, most plots being less than an acre.

We got in our car, and inched our way back to the highway. We continued our clockwise tour along the perimeter, and bought a bottle of water at a store. I spied one lonely bottle in a corner, which cost half as much as at the bar in the hotel, and tasted twice as good, following our walk. I asked as if there was a restroom, and the clerk said no. That was my license to go behind a tree. As I was "inspecting" the local fauna, I noticed that *South Sea Islanders have a distinctive way of walking, deliberate but practical.* Perhaps it is characteristic of the tropics.

We came into the hotel area on the east side of the island, where the tourist shops are thicker, and scuba shops, and artists' showrooms, and black pearl shops are everywhere. Soon we came to the road through the center of the island, past the largest of the excavated marae on Mo'orea, and the belvedere. The road starts out prosperously, past a fish farming experiment, and some larger farms, pineapple and other things. We arrived at the marae, which had been first measured in the modern era by Kenneth Emory, and then carefully excavated by RC Green. I read every line on the explanation while Mary Ann went below to explore. The archeologists believe this was the site of archery contests, about the same time knights were jousting in England and France. Then I went down to the lower platform. It was all in the woods, but when in use was clear between the platforms, they believe.

We got in the car, and went on a serpentine road up to the belvedere. It was recently black-topped, and if traffic gets very heavy there they can set up a body shop right there to unbend fenders. As it was there was a sandwich place right there, and I got a *croque monsuier* and Mary Ann had a double dip ice cream. The view there is great – you can see into the two bays, Cook's Bay and Oponahue Bay – on the east side of the island.

We went the two miles or so to the parking lot, parked the car, gave the papers to Conchita, who went out and checked it, came back and gave me the form to sign, a custom I am beginning to find irksome. Those administering the questionnaires are sensitive as to whether or not you are having a good time, and you are more likely to be pressed to fill them in if you are.

When we turned the car in I decided to get in some snorkeling. I came in, in about 20 minutes or half an hour, and took a nap.

That evening we were scheduled to go to the Tiki Village for a show and Polynesian feast. We were led to the village, the current domicile for the producers of the play, our entertainment for the evening. They showed us the various things that went on in a village: a tattoo parlor, and a craft shop operated by the fiancée of the man guiding us. I was standing quite near her, and we looked at each other and she asked, "Are you grandpapa?" And I said yes, and she asked, "Where are you from?" I couldn't think of the right answer (USA, Atlanta, Georgia?). Mary Ann said something, "Atlanta" I think. The spell was broken. Later she was the lead in the play.

We went in and were seated at a table for four with a young couple on their honeymoon, who were scuba divers, and had been down 80 feet that afternoon. We took the Polynesian line for the buffet dinner and it was very good, but I wouldn't have come 8000 miles just for that. There was a lot of pork.

During dinner they showed us how to tie a pareu. Then we went out to the theater again, and the drama unfolded. The men leap and posture, and the girls jiggle their hips, in time to the music. There was a flaming baton episode, and six men twirled the flaming batons at one time. Two of them exchanged flaming batons, throwing them thirty feet in the air simultaneously. It was beautiful in the dark, with the circles of fire. We'd been to enough productions by now to recognize a few of the songs. We got back to our bungalow at 11:00, our late night of the tour.

That evening our entertainment was pareu tying – that is, how to tie the corners of a 6 foot by 3 foot rectangular piece of cloth to form a decent covering for one's body, either male or female. There are seven essentially different ways to do this, apparently.

We wandered back and tried to locate the Southern Cross. A security man came by in a motorized cart, and we asked him if he could locate it. He understood the question, and the after several minutes and looking at several possibilities he showed us four stars. Looking at the chart at home now I am not certain he had it. *This property of Polynesians is something that dawns on you after a while – they tell you what you want to hear.* Then we went to bed.

September 1

The next morning was bright, and after admiring the sunrise over Tahiti, on the beach 50 feet from our front porch, we went to our elegant breakfast. As we passed the chapel, a Tahitian wedding was being celebrated, for a young Japanese couple. Attending were 12+/- Polynesians, a few tourists, and a Polynesian priest. Mary Ann doesn't think these weddings have legal status. The weddings are designed for the tourist trade. There were three of them this morning.

After the wedding we went on our beach walk. There were two Polynesian girls bouncing in the water, laughing and talking.

September 2

In the morning we were scheduled to fly from Mo'orea to Pape'ete. Tahiti was beautiful across the Sea of the Moon. (I now know the name of the body of water.) Tahiti's profile is distinctive, as are those of Mo'orea and Bora Bora. We have watched the light patterns on all of them. They change by the minute.

They came to pick up our bags, and deliver us to the airport. The flight is 15 minutes in duration, though we had to wait 20 minutes or so for it. We got organized, walked up and caught the local bus, called "Le Truck." They hold perhaps 16 people, and one comes along every 10 minutes or so. We picked up a lot of school children, and others, before being let out downtown.

September 3

The next morning we woke up about 6:30 AM, went out for a brief moment to watch the effect of the sunrise on Mo'orea, and down to breakfast with the mynah birds and a few young French types. At 10:00 we were scheduled to go on the circle of Tahiti tour.

We started out in a nice new van, and picked up four more passengers, making our total seven. The first place we went was the Museum of Tahiti and Her Islands. After we turned off the perimeter road we went through a commercial tropical fruit area. Most of the fruit we have eaten was growing in great profusion alongside the road. After a mile or so we came to the museum, a one-story building covering about an acre. There were large tikis in the courtyard, and the entrance area had an extensive sales room. It cost $10 to get in.

I was interested in the question of how fish hooks were used for dating, and skipped the chronological presentation of the museum's displays to get to that. I asked the attendant where the fish hooks were, and he said, "All along here," and then I asked if it explained how they are used for dating, and he said no. That wasn't quite true, the displays showed three phases

All three were carved from shells and bone. All of the displays were in French and English, and there were several main divisions of the history of the islands, with which I was somewhat familiar from my reading. In addition to the artifacts unearthed by the diggers, there were several journals by the missionaries, reconstructing of ships, many early photographs, a history of the Polynesian battalion in WWII, a chart of the genealogy of the Pomares, with portraits, and many other things.

Later we visited a park centered around some grottos. In two places the trail split into a slightly perilous and a safer option. The peril stemmed from dripping water flowing over stone steps on the path. I took the high road, but was cautious. After we had completed it, there was a disturbance, our guide came running up, and said that one of the party of four in our tour had fallen, and dislocated his shoulder. The French girl on our tour, a nurse, took two tablets from her kit, shook them up in water and made him drink it.

Our guide jumped in the van and drove off to summon an ambulance. We waited until a "truck" came along to take the other members of the foursome back to Pape'ete. Our next stop was the Botanical Garden adjacent to the Gauguin Museum, and then the Gauguin Museum itself. The Botanical Garden is famous, and deservedly

Paul Gaughin Museum

so. It was started by a dropout professor from MIT, Harrison Smith, in 1919. There are lots of big trees of all sorts, and various botanical zones juxtaposed.

Our tour guide had allotted an hour for the two, the garden and the Gauguin Museum. The museum is comparable in quality with the earlier museum. There was a hand-written letter by Gauguin, etc. There were two or three original paintings, nothing major, and reproductions of the majors (The originals are in Paris.). The portrait of his first Tahitian wife, who was from 5 miles up the road, was there in several places, and there was a nice scale model of his house, which had once been located in this very spot.

There was also a room devoted to Jules Verne, and it looked like a complete set of some magazine/newspaper that many of his books first appeared in, in serialized form. They were tied in bundles stacked against the wall. There was a mock-up of Captain Nemo's cockpit, etc. I don't know the connection of Jules Verne with Tahiti, but of course, the South Sea Island bubble was a force in French history, whose influence is still present.

After lunch, we went on the pier again, and saw dozens of jackfish, blue and grey, two feet or more in length. They were very active in the ¼ acre pen at the end of the dock in which there were two frightening-looking moray eels, one of them at least six feet long and four inches across. I tried to be conversational with the French girl, and learned she was from Montreux, Switzerland, but had come from France. She enjoyed talking to the guide, who ate separately, in French, but less so to us in English.

Then we got in the van and continued our perimeter ride. There were numerous small villages as we approached the neck of land between Tahiti Nui and Tahiti Iti, and busses transporting children, and people doing they do in the graceful rhythm of Polynesia. We passed the militia compound and our guide explained the conditions for military service, and that many young men joined because of the high rate of unemployment, around 20%.

On the road there was a construction spot where a landslide had wiped out the road two years ago. We pulled off to view the blowholes, which are tunnels in the lava rock that extend down to the seashore, so that the incoming tide forces air through the tunnels. We stood on the edge of the road and listened to the blasts of air coming out of the upper end, and then crossed the road to watch the surf against the rocks. There were impressive wave geysers with sprays 20 feet high. Then we got back in the van, and I was looking out into the Pacific, where I saw a whale leap out of the water about a mile away. We stopped, and could see disturbances in the water, perhaps their tails, but no real jumps like the first one.

We went on and stopped at a lighthouse designed by Robert Louis Stevenson's father, at a point which contained a memorial to the first protestant missionaries who landed at that point.

Lighthouse designed by R.L. Stevenson's father

September 4? 5? *(when the International Date Line is involved, it's harder to tell)*

Our departure for home was scheduled for 12:45. When we were called, walked out to the plane, we found that we were across the aisle from each other, and there was no remedy since the plane was full. The New Zealand meals were pretty good, with vine-ripened fruit. We both slept some, missed the movie ("Hamlet" directed by Kenneth Branaugh).

We arrived in LA, exactly on time, and had to wait to get our bags. Then we rushed through customs and onto the flight back to Atlanta. We were assured our bags would make the transfer, but they didn't.

After being assured that our luggage would be delivered to our home the next day (which it was), we boarded the shuttle to Athens, listening to the Braves game most of the way, and arriving in the middle of the night. At home at last. Everything looked good, and we crashed.

The books *Typee* (1846) and *Omoo* (1847) by Herman Melville introduced me to Tahiti when I was 14 years old. These books centered on two aspects of Tahiti: the nature of the inhabitants as they evolved in their natural surroundings, and the effects their new visitors had on them. (I shall ignore a modern phenomenon, the use by the French of limited visits by outsiders as a source of revenue.)

The racial memory of early visits by Americans to Tahiti lingers in the creation of Tahiti-like neighborhoods close to home (such as Hilton Head island).

Mathematical Conclusion (For CCMs Only)

A "FUNCTION" IN MATHEMATIC IS THE SOLUTION TO A POLYNOMIAL EQUATION. If you have complete input, the output determines the function. As it relates to my ongoing attempt to figure out the large questions of humanity through the integration of human nature and the principles of mathematics, the "function" of people is the "Youness of You," that part of you that is completely yours. It is an ever-evolving concept, changing over time with new experiences. The function itself is like a black box on an airplane. It can only be recalled and determined in retrospect.

The LLLP of the CCM is determined by the many factors which make up the LLLP. My own functionality was changed by all of these trips, especially those which involved discovering bits of my past and my family history, in Canada and Ireland. Tahiti, and the idea of Tahiti, has played into my LLLP in multiple ways. When I was a child I was entranced with the writing of Herman Melville. Later I was drawn to the art of Paul Gauguin. These influences mixed with Hollywood depictions of the island chain and formed a lasting impression in the mind of this CCM. My experiences in Tahiti lived up to their expectations, and in fact surpassed them.

As a CCM, throughout this quest across the globe, I have attempted to define cultures, the find the root of the "Themness of Them," and look for the factors which gave Them their Themness. One of the largest factors making up their Themness is the relationship between the people and the land. It has often been stated, in various ways that "The land makes the man and the man makes the land." There's some undeniable truth to this axiom. For example, in coastal countries where fishing constitutes a large part of the inhabitants' food source and their way of life, you find communal gatherings in the evenings. In Italy, Spain and the south of France, where fishing has been a part of their way of life for centuries, you find that people tend to gather in town squares, like the Corso, to meet with their neighbors, discuss the day's events, etc. However, in more land-based agricultural communities, farmers tend to centrally focus on crafting their local governments to give them a stabilizing influence, to keep order. Raising livestock and growing crops is both labor-intensive and dependent on factors beyond the farmers' control, like the weather. Therefore, the stabilizing influence of a strong local government can help the inhabitants of these cultures to "weather" the lean times. Fishing communities tend to be more open, likely due to the fact that port cities, by their nature, are influenced by the influx of many people from many different areas of the world, all drawn to their ports. They tend to be less needful of strong governance. Tahiti is a shining example of this.

I'M NOT THE ONLY CCM WHO THINKS THIS WAY. To an extent, we all do. We tend to view everything in the world through a similar lens. We have a kind of universal language, a short hand, which is evident when we talk to each other. Even if we're speaking the language of the country where we are, no one around us has a clue what we're saying. We tend to strive for an economy of language, using as few words as possible in order to communicate complicated ideas. Our mode of thought, best exemplified through Reading Proofs, imposes a kind of uniformity on our thought and speech.

CCMs feel that the valuable thing in life isn't money or respect, all the accessories which come along with being a part of a niche group. We feel that the most treasured aspect of life is having the time to be able to concentrate on thinking your own thoughts. It's an absolute necessity when creating new mathematics.

Money is a binary concept. One either has enough or not. Time to process one's thoughts appears binary on the surface, but the truth is there is never enough time for all of the thoughts a CCM wants to think. However, there is more time when one is in the latter stages of life. This is my challenge to the other CCMs out there. Take the time to do it. There's nothing else in life which is as rewarding.

1) Associated with each individual is a life long learning project (LLLP). Each individual has a distinctive learning project, but there are generalities which apply in most cases. For example, one learns to speak, and communicate in other ways, at a certain age. There are exceptional individuals who don't, but they are not considered normal.
   The learning process evolves over time, more or less cumulatively, in the sense that one doesn't forget what one has learned.

2) Much of the evolution of the life long learning project is directed by teachers. Two types exist, those with whom an individual has physical contact, and those whose influence is by means of artifacts such as books and other methods of communication.

3) A mathematician is an individual who creates sentences which cannot possibly be interpreted in two different ways. Originally such sentences dealt with the natural numbers, but over time they evolved into statements involving irrational numbers and ideas that such numbers led to. These include geometry, both Euclidian and non-Euclidian, topology and other things.
   These mathematical sentences lead to proofs, which are sequences of sentences submitted to other mathematicians who rule whether they are correct or not. If the sequences are unanimously rules correct, the argument is accepted as fact.
   If not accepted, the lack of precision is explained. Such errors can be fatal, or reparable. Both cases have occurred.

Explanatory Note About Teaching

I WAS TOLD AT A YOUNG AGE BY MY FATHER THAT I WAS BORN TO BE A TEACHER. This was reinforced by a quotation from Chaucer which was engraved on an outside wall of my high school. "Gladly would he learn, and gladly teach."

The teachers of an individual can be separated into two classes: those encountered personally, and those whose influence is transmitted by artifacts – books, poems, art, etc.

In most cases the first teachers one encounters are one's mother and father. They impart sounds and words. The experience of the life long learning process (LLLP) is evolutionary, and as time goes by, one's influential teachers change with circumstances.

EACH INDIVIDUAL ENGAGES IN A LIFE LONG LEARNING PROCESS WHICH EVOLVES WITH AGE. The early stages are taken up with learning to communicate with others, eventually leading to the contribution to society by means of which one is supported.

Eventually one retires, and is therefore free to attempt to learn one's own true character. Those who attain an elderly age have learned to adapt to the circumstances which have been dealt. These can be of several types, including the geography of one's location, the individuals with whom one is in contact, the sources of one's own entertainment, and so on.

The curiosity to know what's coming next is conducive to longer life, and a humorous acceptance of what turns up is helpful.

Summarizing Entire Cultures

As a CCM, my fraternity tends to look for grand answers to complex questions. As this trait applies to travel it means that I, and my fellow CCMs, try to figure out each country's contribution to the large world society.

ITALY (ROME) gave us the city-state.

FRANCE gave us the revolutionary idea of "liberty, equality, fraternity."

GREAT BRITAIN gave us the rules of how a society could run with orderly precision. The strength of the British Empire stemmed from its innate orderliness.

To that end, I, as any self-respecting CCM would, am adding philosophical asides to this narrative, summarizations of entire cultures in bite-sized chunks.

CCMs Throughout History

I'M NOT THE FIRST CCM, NOR WILL I BE THE LAST. Early CCMs were always known as mathematicians. Sometimes they went by other names, but the basics were the same. Even something as seemingly commonplace as accurate bookkeeping, to be done correctly, required at least some CCM skills. One popular version of historical CCMs were land surveyors. To precisely survey land one had to know trigonometry. Then, as now, it was a specialized field with only a very few members. Many were celebrated: surveyors of famous battles, settlers of land disputes. The first five presidents of the University of Georgia were all minor-league CCMs. They could keep the books.

This Story Represents What The World Thinks Of Americans

We had an airport shuttle bus driver named Terry. We were headed toward Tahiti, having recently come back from Wales. When we told Terry about our time in Wales, he launched into a Welsh story of his own…Terry's great-grandfather emigrated, leaving behind a big, stone house in Wales, and his grandfather's two sons, a mason and a carpenter, reproduced it in the middle of Ohio. All this happened in 1816 and the years following. Then the old man's immediate family, which contained some literate clergymen, all died young, so sometime after 1900 he tore the house down and built a wooden house. The stone house, had it survived, would have been the most historic building in the area. Terry's uncle went back to Wales when the head of the family there died, and went to the original stone house, and knocked at the door. He was met by one of the daughters, who immediately went to the fireplace mantel, got a large knife, and stabbed a dog who was sitting there through the heart, saying, "That's what I will do to you if you ever set foot on this property again." So his uncle went to the lawyers, and after a suitable amount of litigation, got a share of the estate due the Americans.

www.ingramcontent.com/pod-product-compliance
Lightning Source LLC
LaVergne TN
LVHW052303100826
845147LV00006B/666

* 9 7 8 1 7 3 2 6 1 8 0 8 4 *